Dispatches from the Ark

Pages from A Pet Psychic's Notebook

by Suzan Vaughn

Published by:
Medium Masters Publishing
P.O. Box 3702
San Luis Obispo, California 93403-3702
www.telepathictalk.com

Cover art by Jan Dungan

© 2008 by Suzan Vaughn
ISBN 13: 978-0-9814772-0-6

Dedication

To Rusti, my regal chow chow, who taught me what "animal companion" really means and lifted me up to a higher level of reverence for all life.

I couldn't love you more, my little red dog.

Acknowledgments

Bringing *Dispatches from the Ark* to you, dear reader, has been a five-year process. Originally titled *How Spirit Nudged Me Kicking and Screaming into the Inspiring World of Interspecies Communication*, this book was born of a journey filled with both trepidation and light, with many friends helping me along the way.

The animals and people who willingly shared their stories are at the top of my thank-you list. I'm grateful that they trusted me to bring through their important messages.

Dispatches from the Ark started out as a stack of separate stories that later became chapters for a book-length manuscript, thanks in great part to my earliest inspiration and editor, Diana Somerville, my friend and the author of *Inside Out/Down Under*. Suzan Bick and Jody Berman (of Berman Editorial) went on to help with organization and editing.

My friend and final editor, Vicki Hanson (of Hanson Writing & Editing), marked final text drafts with great care, handled chapter graphics, and formatted the book for print, inspiring me along the way with her own enthusiasm for the project. Her husband, Nels, provided valuable suggestions for the book's title and section heads—and communicated successfully with his cats using some of the techniques I describe. The first time Vicki sent me a glimpse of my words in real book form, I responded to her e-mail with an intense series of chills up and down my spine, a rush of emotion, and tears—Heaven didn't want me to miss the message that I was, after all, on the right track.

First among those whose help came long before my book began to take shape is my mother, Janice Rodgers. Her love, support, and contagious sense of humor are so very dear to me, and she has been open enough to "see" with her heart and through the love of her Higher Sources. I thank her for being always my champion. Bless her for seeing the magic in a homeless, bedraggled chow chow and for encouraging me to adopt Rusti.

Bob, my faithful husband, deserves an affection-filled embrace for his quiet encouragement. He steadily picks up the workload of other joint projects when I spend time on the book, and I appreciate it beyond measure. A hug from him can transform my world.

My good friend and traveling companion, Sir Francis Grossi, has always been a steady support to me, and I thank him as well.

Finally, a wink and a nod go to the Wise Women of the Pacific Northwest: Diana, Marilyn, Ruth, Barbara, Jan, Carol, Laura, and Julia. Other wise women on my team there included Pepper, Gail, Kristine, Hope, Kirsten, Cherise, and Carleen. All of these women are truly the best of the Northwest, and have helped me see the best in myself. ☀

Contents

Preface

"Come forth into the light of things,
Let Nature be your teacher."
~ William Wordsworth (1770 – 1850)

Anyone who has ever loved an animal knows a kind of love that's unconditional and inspiring. In the face of neglect, abandonment, abuse, and even death at the hands of humans, other species still learn to trust and love again. The truth is that the needs of our pets and other creatures are simple and straightforward, and if we learn how to listen to them we can help forge deep and fulfilling relationships that teach us a great deal about how to treat each other.

This book is about reverence for, and communication with, all life, from the smallest insect to the giant elephant. What if, instead of filling our homes, offices, and environments with poisons to rid us of "pests," we could simply ask these tiny creatures to find a more suitable home? What if we could question a cat about her refusal to use the litter box? What if we could project a calm energy over a household of troubled rescue dogs that would help them overcome their fear of abandonment? I'm here to say we can. I've done all these things.

My notebook is also more than a manual about how to talk to animals. That book has already been written a number of times. I'm writing to chronicle my personal journey of change from one career to another within my chosen field of communication and to show the reader that intention, practice, dedication, and spiritual connection are what it takes to commune with all forms of life.

Almost every book I've read on how to talk to animals says anyone can do it. Most of the authors claim to have had the gift either from earliest childhood or as a miraculous revelation. Not me.

My early inclinations were discouraged and forgotten. I had to start from scratch. And even though I practiced psychic counseling "on the side" for many years by offering private sessions to people, I was reluctant to declare my new profession as a pet and people psychic counselor. It was far less acceptable to loved ones, friends, and fans than my career as news anchor, producer, and talk show host. The transition was a difficult redefinition for my ego. The road to declaring my own truth, and embracing self-acceptance in the face of the disapproval of those I held most dear, was and continues to be a long and arduous one.

My work in animal and interspecies communication came 15 years after I began my practice of daily meditation, study, and psychic counseling with people. With a strong desire to exit the news business following the events of 9/11, I clearly let my Higher Sources know that what I needed was work that inspired others.

Enter the animals. Their stories were moving, heart-wrenching, and full of a depth of love that brought tears to my eyes.

I wrote this book because it is my contention that we need to clean up our relationships with other species. We can start that process by tuning in to them and finding out what they're trying to tell us.

My life's work has always been about communication, so it was a natural extension of that work to delve into the world of telepathic communication. I wanted to find out how it worked, how to use it effectively, how to identify its unique offerings and limitations, and ultimately how to introduce others to this ancient mind-to-mind way of conversing. I was fascinated by its promise as a means of communicating between species and between physical and non-physical entities. It's exciting to practice a form of contact that transcends time, space, species, and geographic boundaries.

Of course I'm not the first explorer to experiment with the use of telepathy in communicating with animals. Rupert Sheldrake, biologist and author of more than 75 scientific papers and 10 books, has studied how a dog knows when its human is about to return home unexpectedly, and why so many animals escaped the deadly 2004 Asian tsunami.

After five years of extensive research involving thousands of people who own and work with animals, Sheldrake conclusively proved what many people who live closely with animals already know: There is a strong connection between humans and animals that lies beyond present-day scientific understanding.

In *A New Science of Life: The Hypothesis of Morphic Resonance,* Sheldrake observes that when laboratory rats in one place have learned how to navigate a new maze, rats elsewhere in the world seem to learn it more easily. He describes this process as "morphic resonance"—past forms and behaviors of organisms influencing other organisms in the present through direct connections across time and space.

A review of 20 years of mental telepathy research published in January 1994 in the *Psychological Bulletin* not only shows significant clinical evidence that telepathy exists, but also reveals surprising connections between artists and psychic abilities. Cornell University professor of psychology Daryl J. Bem co-authored the article with the late University of Edinburgh parapsychologist Charles Honorton, who conducted most of the experiments.

"Taken with earlier studies, the probability that the results could have occurred by chance is less than one in a billion," Bem writes.

There is also a rapidly growing body of literature on telepathic animal communication, and my own experiences have validated everything I've read on the subject.

My first communication career was much more conventional than talking to animals. Twenty-five years as a broadcast and print journalist, coupled with years in meditation, prayer, and spiritual practice, and degrees in both psychology and communication, eventually resulted in becoming captivated by this ancient kind of conversing, which included practitioners speaking not only with comatose patients but with animals, non-physical Teachers, and even angelic Guides.

I came to believe that telepathic communication enables us to more fully empathize by using our natural ability to sense the thoughts, feelings, images, ideas, and sensations of another being without the spoken word. Yet just as language requires constant diligence when it comes to making sure the message we are sending is received in the way it's intended, telepathic communication also requires due diligence and clarity.

The best practitioners of telepathy experience a quality of loving compassion and an appreciation for the plight of others, including our animal companions, as a result of this dialogue that emanates from the heart, soul, and spirit. We come to feel and to know, on a deep and profound level, that we are all from the same spiritual source. This kind of communication opens us up to the deepest possible connection with all other living beings, whether they are the same species or not.

Through telepathy, we can better hear the language of the soul—the whisper that becomes more recognizable as it gently guides us through the maze of physical existence. This is the kind of communication that tells us, before the phone rings and before we pick up the receiver, who is on the other end of the line; that warns us not to board that airplane or get into this elevator; that rattles a parent to the core when an absent child is hurt or endangered.

We're all born with the ability to send and receive telepathic messages. It's just a matter of choosing to develop the skills needed to effectively make use of telepathy on a day-to-day basis.

In my professional practice today, I am an interpreter and translator of telepathic messages. I use this form of communication, this developed skill, to speak to God/Goddess, to my own soul, to the soul of other travelers in this physical world who seek my counsel, to animals of all kinds, and to all non-verbal living things.

It is my hope that as I share my story you will be inspired, comforted, and blessed. May these words bring you closer to your own soul and to the Sacred Divine. ❄

Section I

First Signals

"All truths are easy to understand once they are discovered; the point is to discover them."

~ *Galileo Galilei (1564 – 1642)*
Italian astronomer and physicist

1

My Journey Begins

I wish I could say that a beautiful, angelic vision in white floated around my bedroom ceiling one night, miraculously dropping the psychic gift into my head. If it had happened that way I'd have a more dramatic story to tell about coming to realize my psychic abilities.

In fact, redeveloping those talents took work, study, and practice. Children are born with these sixth senses, but through social conditioning, disapproval, and denial, they're often lost and have to be rediscovered. That's my story, and one I share with many people.

The day I found out that my Guides considered me a potential candidate to help people and their pets through the use of telepathic communication was a mystical experience in itself that took place during my twice-yearly expedition to see Patty Hatton, my psychic and friend in Cambria, California.

Patty knew she had the gift of insight in early childhood. Fortunate enough to be part of a family of psychics who didn't discourage her talents, she had fine-tuned her abilities until she was a highly sought-after medium. People came from the far reaches of the United States to have a reading with her; others asked for her help by mail. *What a wonderful gift she's been given*, I thought to myself as I drove north. *It would be a privilege and an honor to do such work.*

I remembered that in an earlier session Patty had told me someone would share my small house, and it would be a significant relationship. Unable to imagine such an arrangement, I thought for sure she must be wrong. Because she said it would be someone who would need my help, I ran through a list in my head of all the needy people I could think of, deciding how I would deflect their efforts to invade my small living space.

But her accurate prediction turned out not to involve a

person at all, I discovered, when Rusti came to live with me six months later. A cat person, I had never owned a dog nor even considered it, and this turn of events was something I could never have predicted. The little red chow chow became a significant part of my life, appearing on "The Suzan Vaughn" TV show as my sidekick, then as an important third animal player in my two-cat household. Not only had Patty predicted Rusti's arrival, she had also told me she saw me on television, which at the time I found exciting but unlikely.

It was a beautiful day when she gave me the news. The small Plymouth I drove followed a winding coastal route alongside my adored Pacific Ocean as the pungent odor of spring kelp drying on the beach sand blew through the open windows. Thick humidity hung in the air, making my hair curly, and I breathed in the spray. It was a mild, sunny day—cooperative weather for my eagerly anticipated appointment.

Patty seemed to tune right into my thoughts soon after our session began. After silently connecting with her Guides, she told me, "You know, you could do this work. The Teachers say you come of good counsel." I smiled as I remembered thinking what an honor and a thrill it would be to have her gift of insight while driving to see her just a short while earlier.

As usual the session was a good one, with Patty accurately predicting things I could never have foreseen and didn't even understand at the time. She told me of relationships ending and beginning, of health issues, and of changes at work and in my household.

As I drove home, my rational mind began sifting through the information Patty had brought through. What would it be like to bring comfort and guidance to people from their Higher Sources? Had I studied enough, practiced enough? Was I good enough? What background would qualify me to bring this kind of service to people? I was humbled by these thoughts.

Over the next months, I philosophized, intellectualized, researched, and examined exactly what it would take and what it would mean for me to be a psychic counselor. I already knew my life's purpose was tied to psychology and communication, the disciplines associated with my educational degrees, and the thought of offering a new kind of communication service was inspiring.

I had already spent some 15 years in the study of

metaphysical phenomenon, with an early devotion to the *Seth Materials,* the writings of Jane Roberts. Roberts and her husband, Robert Butts, had produced a series of books with Seth, who described himself as "an intelligence residing outside of time and space." Seth was channeled by Jane Roberts from 1963 until her death in 1984. After my good friend Sharon gave me the first Seth volume, the thought of communicating with other realms of existence fascinated and inspired me, and I devoured the entire collection one book after another.

During those years, I read extensively about spirituality, psychic phenomena, scientific attempts to quantify telepathy, and the work of other psychics. But once I heard what Patty had to say, it became more personal: I shifted to a more conscientious practice of my daily meditation and began to practice on willing clients on the weekends.

Early on, I worked on the first challenge facing any new psychic: Trusting the messages, feelings, pictures, smells, and other sense data I got from my Guides, then having the courage to translate what I was feeling out loud. Eventually I discovered that this same kind of communication worked like a charm with animals.

As mediums, we are not meant to judge the words or feelings that come through, simply to pass them on. Two women who came to my table at a psychic fair helped me learn that lesson in trust.

They expectantly sat down at the table in front of me where my signed announced "Messages from Your Teachers, Guides, Pets, or Loved Ones on the Other Side," hoping to hear from a dear friend who had recently departed.

Almost immediately I could sense the presence of a relatively young man from the other side who wanted to be there with the women. As is sometimes the case, he beamed with love for them but had little else to say.

I concentrated. I focused. But I came up blank, except for one sentence that I kept shooing away like an annoying fly.

"I'm sorry," I said finally, sharing what I knew would be their mutual disappointment. "He seems to be a man of few words, although his feeling of love for the two of you is profound."

They looked dejected, although they confirmed that he was indeed not much of a talker.

I wanted to make it up to them. "Well, okay," I said, "there is *one* thing that keeps coming through, although I'm not sure it's accurate."

A hopeful spark lit their faces.

"He's saying, 'You go, girls!'"

With that, the two women jumped up from their chairs simultaneously, exclaiming in unison, "That's *him!*"

Blasted with my first dramatic lesson in allowing the information to come through unfiltered, I had again tiptoed over one of the obstacles for the practicing psychic: trusting what comes through.

Other early successes like this one told me that my psychic advisor was right: I *could* do this work, and I *could* provide clients with helpful information and counseling. So in 1995, I began offering readings after work and on weekends on a more regular basis.

I soon found that, in most ways, life as a psychic is not very different from life as a non-psychic. Many people don't quite grasp that—especially men who may be considering dating you, or new acquaintances sizing you up as a potential dinner guest.

But it's not as if your Guides give you any more clues about what's going to happen in your own life than they do to anyone else, and you're not immune to experiencing the same painful emotions as the rest of the population. On the other hand, we all get clues, messages, and warnings when we're on the wrong path. Like small, annoying chest pains that eventually become a heart attack if we continue smoking.

Psychics are regular folks who don't, for the most part, wear turbans, carry crystal balls, or don sparkly robes, except on Halloween. It might be easier to spot a psychic if we went around clothed in unconventional garb, but we've been persecuted in other lifetimes for using and teaching our mind-to-mind communication and if our abilities are genuine many of us are a bit reserved about them.

As in all nurturing professions, the work life of a psychic counselor can be stressful. Many clients are emotionally distressed, sometimes holding in, or letting go of, an avalanche of fear and anger. I once had a male client who was so angry that I practically devolved into a fetal position for three days after his appointment because I was too new in the business to know how to shield myself from his rage.

For the conscientious psychic, it takes time and dedication to do good work on a client's behalf. When you consult a psychic, you should be hiring a professional counselor and communicator who can offer insight, wisdom, sound advice, motivation, and empathy, along with a wide range of listening, interpreting, and speaking skills that include telepathic communication. (If instead your psychic focuses on asking for lots of money to remove a negative "spell" or a dark cloud hovering over you, zip up your pocketbook and sprint rapidly in the opposite direction.)

As with any professional U-turn, even though intellectually I knew undertaking a new career would be challenging, I discovered the nuances of those challenges one by one. Psychics have to visit a psychic to get more insight on their own futures. So when a series of events gently nudged me in the direction of becoming a full-time professional psychic counselor, I reluctantly embraced the challenge.

Fed up and spiritually drained from reporting on the latest tragedy of the day as a news broadcaster, I fell in love with a man who lived in a small Washington town and married him. With his support, I saw an opportunity to spread my wings in a more inspiring professional direction.

Who can argue with the gift of freedom to pursue a more meaningful vocation? Yet while it all sounds delicious on paper, that kind of freedom can also be daunting. In fact I was gently nudged and carried, silently kicking and screaming, into my new vocation—the work of my Soul-level Guides.

Yet little by little, bit by bit, the thick restrictive tethers of needing approval from outside sources loosened, my psychic experiences built up personally undeniable empirical evidence, and a steady stream of clients began seeking me out, asking for my help. ☀

2

Domesticating Rusti

I did not grow up with animals.

My mother was deathly afraid of every species of critter, except for a few little turtles we kept in a tabletop habitat for a short time when I was small. Mom's early childhood in Las Cruces, New Mexico—one in which wild cats were thrown at her as a joke by her older brother, puppies were routinely drowned if unwanted, and horses were considered necessary equipment to plow the fields of neighboring farms—did not make her fond of animals.

Few people understood Mom's fear and continually tried to force their pets on her, saying, "Oh, he won't bite." These well-meaning folks made her paranoia worse, and the scent of Mom's fear often provoked an aggressive response in the animals.

But I always liked animals, especially other people's pets in our middle-class Southern California neighborhood.

Heidi, a big German shepherd who lived next door, was good at her job of guarding her human companion's house. Darlene was a colorful character who worked nights as a honky-tonk piano player at a local bar, so Heidi watched over the place at night and while Darlene slept during the daytime.

A seven-foot block wall fence separated our backyard from Darlene's. It was my job to take out the trash and Heidi barked up a storm whenever I went out there and opened the gate. She would jump so high I could see the top of her head over the fence.

I always spoke to her calmly, telling her, "It's all right, Heidi. It's only me." Then her bark would become one of greeting, actually changing in tone and intensity.

Due to adult worries about Heidi's size and ferocity, we never actually met in person, but we were always friends.

It wasn't until I was in my early twenties, when I was living in Orange, California, that cats became a constant part of my household. As soon as I had my first apartment where animals were allowed, I marched right down to the local humane society and picked out a pair: Batgirl (so named because she was a black and white tuxedo cat with mask-like markings) and Doc (part of a litter of kitties that included Hickory and Dickory).

At the time I never considered bringing a dog into my home. When people told me dogs made good companions I thought to myself, *They can't carry on a conversation. How can something that can't talk be a good companion?* I just didn't understand *how* animals communicated, and although I really liked my two new cats, I thought a relationship with them would mostly be fun and entertaining.

The depth of feeling animal lovers experience with their animal companions was simply outside of my limited experience until my first real dog relationship more than 10 years later. I was living on California's Central Coast when Rusti taught me how extraordinary that bond can be.

The road to having a dog in my life was certainly unforeseen, but when it finally happened it started me down the path to becoming an animal communicator.

*   *   *

One August night around midnight, in the middle of a work week, a tremendous ruckus outside my bedroom window woke me up. Angry at my sleep being interrupted, I peered out the window to see a pack of dogs following a single red chow chow. I cursed the unknown chow's people under my breath, assuming they hadn't gotten their dog spayed, then tried to get back to sleep as the noisy pack continued down the middle of the street.

Later that month, on a pre-dawn Wednesday a few minutes before 3 a.m., my eyes flew open, anticipating the regular ring of the alarm clock.

Hitting the off button to avoid the loud buzzing that could catapult me out of a pleasantly dreamy reverie, I lay still in my cozy bed, listening intently to a distant sound I knew I'd heard before but couldn't quite identify. It seemed to be coming from the other side of the house, maybe the porch. As I focused my attention, I suddenly realized what it was—the muffled sound of snoring! Alarmed, I arose quietly, tiptoeing toward the front door to investigate, but the snoring stopped just as my feet touched the floor.

For the next two weeks, the same sound would wake me up before dawn and then stop as soon as I turned off the alarm or got out of bed.

I telephoned my mother to tell her about these weird happenings.

She was puzzled too. "That's very strange," she said. "Do you feel you're in any kind of danger?"

I assured her I didn't think so, but the possibility of an unwanted stranger making himself at home on my porch did make me uneasy.

At least another two weeks went by before I heard the sound again. There it was, in the early hours of the morning—unmistakable snoring. The minute the alarm went off or my feet hit the floor, the sound immediately stopped.

About the same time, I started noticing a mangy rust-colored dog at the Grange Hall across the street watching me when I left for work. She started showing up every morning, keeping at least 50 feet between us at all times. Obviously a chow with her perky, bear-like ears, she had sprigs of hair poking out here and there and the trademark black tongue. Her fur was matted, with big clumps missing, and she scratched constantly. She looked exhausted.

The difficulty of her situation began to invade my thoughts. After about a week, her pitiful, drooping appearance finally got to me, so I bought two cheeseburgers on the way home from work and left them on the porch of the Grange Hall. As I drove my car through the parking lot, I spotted the chow hiding in the bushes. After moving the cheeseburgers closer to her on the dirt, I got back in my car to watch. She was motionless.

I drove home, parked my car, and went inside to my front window. The cheeseburgers stayed untouched. I walked across the street and opened the food up to further entice her with the smell, but she stayed hidden. I went back home and watched out the window to see if the skittish stray would venture out.

I waited a long time, finally giving up my window seat, resolving to check on her periodically instead. But the chow waited until dark before she stealthily sneaked up on those burgers and devoured them.

Few people knew anything about the wild red dog when I inquired around the neighborhood.

"I feed her sometimes," one soft-hearted animal lover told me. "Some people say her master was taken away to a convalescent home by ambulance. You know, chows are one-person dogs. I'm sure she was reluctant to let anyone else take her."

Plenty of people had tried. After contacting several animal rescue agencies, I learned that a number of workers had attempted to trap her, using food to try to lure her into different enclosures. But she was extremely wary and had eluded Animal Services officers for two years.

One morning I crept out of bed again, trying to find out where the mysterious snoring was coming from. The moment I looked out the front door, I saw the chow dart out from under my house and run across the street. Finally, I had discovered the source of the snoring! Each day after that, just before the alarm went off at three, I listened for the familiar sound. But the dog was restless and always on guard, so I didn't hear her often. In fact, she had a way of disappearing. At times I could look straight at her when she was across the street in the bushes and not see her at all. I caught glimpses of her only when she moved.

I felt bad for her and began leaving food for her regularly across the street after I learned she was staying under my house. But I was careful not to leave it too close to home. Feeding her at the Grange Hall would tell her she didn't belong to me, I reasoned. I wanted to help her out, but I was a cat person, after all—with no intention of owning a dog.

*　　　*　　　*

In December, a new sound came from under the house— the playful growling of tiny pups.

I could hear them through the floorboards only on occasion, and only when the red mama dog was out in the neighborhood. My heart melted for the struggling chow, whom I had named Rusti. (I had no idea if she was male or female in those standoffish days before the pups came. So I started out calling him/her "That rusty-looking old dog across the street." Eventually, she responded to "Rusty," and when I found out she was female, I reasoned that changing the spelling of her name to end with an "i" instead of a "y" would be enough of a nod to her femininity.)

Vowing to help her as much as she would let me, I bought the best dog food available for a nursing mother, placing it directly under the house so she didn't have to forage far from home. I knew Rusti needed help surviving and nurturing her puppies, and I became committed to helping her at this most vulnerable time, hoping that maybe later on I could get her spayed so she might become adoptable.

By mid-January, I calculated that the pups were about five weeks old. No longer content to stay under my small house, they began following their mother when she ventured out from under the house, much to her dismay—and mine. About the same time, a raging fever related to pneumonia engulfed me. Too weak to go to work, I realized I needed help when after several bedridden days I found myself too weak to stand at the stove long enough to open and heat a can of soup. Thank heaven for *my* mother, who moved in and took care of me until my strength returned. Nurturing was taking place both above and below the floorboards, but Rusti was super skittish.

My little house was situated on a very busy street. Several times Rusti was spooked by movement inside the house, dashing across the pavement with one pup still attached to a teat. Cars slammed on their brakes, and the puppy would drop, disoriented, onto the road. Chaos then ensued as Rusti ran to the other side of the street, barking loudly at the forlorn puppy, urging it back under the house. The situation worried me greatly, and passing motorists had strong opinions about what kind of pet caretaker was related to those pups. More than once, I dragged myself out of my sickbed to address an angry person knocking on my front door.

"Is that your dog out in the street with her puppies? Don't you know they're going to get hit by a car?" they raged, as I, red-eyed and wiped out, tried to explain: No, Rusti didn't belong to me.

Once, my concern for her safety prompted me to block an open crawl space under the front porch that gave her access to the street. I tried to contain her under the house with bricks and wooden structures designed to divert her into the fenced backyard. But her incredible strength enabled her to use her head to break out of anything I constructed. She easily escaped from under the house by simply head-butting the bricks until she reopened the space. Penning her in like that also made her so upset that it eroded some of the tentative trust we were building, and I vowed never to do it again.

With Rusti still far too anxious to come anywhere near me, the assistance I could offer her was limited to food and under-the-house shelter. Forced to turn my attention to what I could do for the pups, I figured I could at least try to make them human-friendly, giving them a chance at a better life.

After a series of antibiotics, I felt well enough to spend a few minutes a day in the sunshine, cooing and cajoling the pups to come out into the yard. Mostly, they stayed nervously under the house, but my efforts were rewarded with glimpses of their cute fluffy manes. After weeks of talking to them, I persuaded two pups to come out to play and check out the dog food and water bowl while Rusti was away. The two bravest, a boy and a girl, ventured out for the first time somewhere between four and five weeks old.

Eventually, I learned that Rusti had given birth to four adorable light brown balls of fur: three females and one male. They looked just like their chow mother, except they were brown instead of red. Still too sick to keep a watchful eye on them, I needed my mother's help to corral them into the backyard when they were accidentally dumped onto the street. Bravely, Mom swallowed her fear, picked them up, and carried them to the backyard, where they scurried under the house. Back inside the house, Mom watched the haggard Rusti pace back and forth across the street. That's when Mom fell in love with a dog for the first time.

I was hoping that I could at least keep the puppies safe for a few more weeks—at six weeks old, I reasoned, I'd be able to find them homes. At about five weeks, three pups came out from under the house to play. The three little furballs were experimenting with eating and drinking from a bowl I provided as a training tool. The fourth pup, a girl, was nowhere to be found.

When the puppies were six weeks old, I rounded up the male. He had been promised to a woman who walked past the house several times a week and had spotted the litter peeking out from under the house. The woman wanted the boy, saying she planned to call him Bear. I screened her as an appropriate placement, made sure her husband was on board with the adoption, and handed little brown Bear over to a very happy couple. The two remaining puppies were taken to Animal Services and found homes immediately. What had happened to the fourth pup was a mystery.

Although handing the puppies over was difficult, I breathed a huge sigh of relief because they were no longer endangered by cars on the busy road. Rusti's take on the situation was quite different. Returning to her hideaway and finding all her children gone that evening put her in a state of panic. Inconsolable, she paced up and down across the street, barking.

She barked loud and long every night for a week, until I was exhausted and unable to function at work.

When I called Animal Services and requested their help, they informed me that they had been after the smart chow for over two years and had never been able to capture her. The dog would head out into an open field whenever their trucks approached. Unable to bribe her with food, no matter how hungry she was, they faced a dilemma: The sheriff's department was taking over county Animal Services, and contracts with the individual cities meant limited service to the town where I lived. New rules meant that unless the residents complained about an animal's situation several times, no action was taken.

Once I knew those rules, I called daily. Finally, Animal Services came out, shot Rusti with a tranquilizer dart, and took her away.

After numerous irate citizen complaints, and two years of trying to lure her into baited traps, the troublesome dog's capture made the paper: "Red Chow Ruckus Ends with a Dart" read the headline in the police beat section. The short article went on to describe her capture and the number of complaints she had racked up over the years. Rusti was safe and off the street for at least a few days because, by law, Animal Services had to keep her three days in case someone wanted to claim her. However, on the third day, she was scheduled for lethal injection.

On day two, I went to the shelter to see if I could move forward with my plan to pay for sterilization, making her more adoptable. I was sure my mother would be supportive of this decision, but much to my surprise she encouraged me to adopt Rusti instead. "There's something special about that dog," she said. I couldn't believe my ears, but I still wasn't convinced. I hadn't checked it out with my landlord.

Skepticism accompanied me to the shelter. When I arrived, I told the officer in charge that I was looking for a specific dog from my neighborhood. He opened the gate and pointed me to the rows of dogs waiting expectantly in cages for new families to claim them. That sad sight depressed me as I walked past the rows of caged dogs. Rusti wasn't there.

"I didn't find the one I'm looking for," I told the officer, "but I know you picked her up just two days ago.

"Maybe you can describe her," he said.

"She's a red chow."

That was all the explanation he needed. "Oh, *that* dog," he groaned. "She's in quarantine and I'm sorry to say, she's not adoptable. A chow that's been wild for two years will never be domesticated," he warned. Then he educated me about the breed's one-person, often aggressive, independent nature.

"But can't I at least see her?" I asked.

He called another officer over and relayed the request. Both were wary of unlocking Rusti's cage and neither wanted to go in. I volunteered but they thought that was a bad idea. Finally, the second officer decided to see if he could get Rusti on a leash. He unlocked the door to the quarantine area. Each cage had an outer area where food and water were offered and a small inside area of cement walls, where a dog could hide out. Although Rusti was the only dog resident in quarantine, she was hidden in the far reaches of the pen where no one could see her.

I approached the chain link gate, reading the card placed outside her pen where the staff had taken notes. "Depressed. Not eating," it said. There was still no dog in sight as we stood looking in, but as I began speaking to the officer, Rusti appeared, coming out of hiding as a response to a familiar voice.

"Wow! That's the first time I've ever seen her react to anything or anyone!" exclaimed the officer. As he went inside the cage, Rusti easily allowed him to put a leash on her and he handed it over to me.

Leading her to the fenced area where people become acquainted with potential new pets, I could tell Rusti was ecstatic to see me, the first familiar person, place, or thing she'd laid eyes on in two days on death row. As I sat down on the pavement, she licked my face and hair and searched frantically for a way out of the pen but continued to come back to me—amazing behavior since she had never come within 20 yards of me before, even while I was feeding her.

Shocked by her friendly behavior and armed with my mother's approval, I decided to try and adopt Rusti, even though Animal Services was against the idea.

"I'll come back to get you tomorrow," I reassured her. Still, the staff was firm that this dog was not adoptable, but I had another card to play—an ace in the hole.

The next day I called the director of Animal Services. We had become acquainted through several radio programs I had produced on animal adoptions, euthanasia, spay and neuter options, and other animal-related topics, so I called in a favor and convinced her to let me give Rusti's adoption a try. My landlord, a dog lover, also agreed to allow me to adopt her.

When I checked Rusti out of doggie death row for good the next day, she was one happy dog. She obeyed simple commands immediately, knew how to walk on a leash, and jumped right into the car. She seemed to know that I had rescued her from doom. I hated the thought of being separated from her within hours of adopting her, but it would be a few more days before we could relax into our new roles at my house.

Our first destination was the groomer's, where help with Rusti's skin problems was top priority. Later that day, I handed her over to the vet for spaying. She was going straight from one cage to another, but even through all the unfamiliar handling she never growled, snapped, or made an aggressive move toward the service providers.

Rusti was groggy and still slightly drugged when I picked her up two days later and brought her home. She seemed shy and standoffish. I laid her gently in a warm, dark place in the house while she recovered from surgery. When she was well enough, her first instinct was to head for the door, scratching on it to be let out. My complying told her she wasn't trapped, and within the hour she returned to scratch on the door to be let back in. Over the next several months, she used me as a safe refuge, hiding behind my legs when other people approached, especially men.

The smaller-than-normal red chow had plenty of issues from living on the street. She was afraid of people, garden hoses, doorways, and loud noises, and cautious about food, even when it was me doing the feeding. For the first five years she lived with me, she never ate her food until I went to bed. She somehow knew to scratch on the door to be let out, and from the very first day, she was fully house-trained.

Rusti prompted my first encounter with a pet psychic who appeared on my weekly television program, "The Suzan

Vaughn Show," which I produced and hosted after finishing my daily radio duties. This guest encouraged me to tell Rusti that I would take care of her for life, which I did. At the prompting of the pet psychic, I also explained to her that her puppies had gone to happy homes. She seemed much calmer and less jumpy after that.

Two months after Rusti came to live with me, we were sitting together on the porch when a woman I'd never seen before pulled up in a pick-up truck.

"I just thought you'd like to know," she called out. "I took a puppy that was wandering around in the street in front of your house a few months ago. She's turned out to be a wonderful asset on my ranch. She fit right in with my other dogs and is a hard worker."

Relieved, I thanked the woman for letting me know and shared the information with Rusti. Her fourth pup had also found a good home!

*   *   *

As the years went by, Rusti traveled a long way down the road to domestication, even though she still hid behind me sometimes. After eight years, she started eating her dinner soon after I put it down, but not until I left the room. After nine, she let me watch.

But even after a decade, she still trotted quickly to the other side of the yard when I pulled out the garden hose and still rushed through suspicious doorways quickly, lest the door be shut on her. She was prone to hide under a desk if she knew it was time for a bath or if the vacuum was being used, but I soothed her fears with kind words and gentle petting and she eventually came around. Always regal, she never jumped on people or offered unsolicited tongue baths.

And now I could easily identify the sound of snoring at the foot of the bed: It was no longer alarming but comforting. It meant that Rusti was nearby sleeping safely, deeply, soundly. Before she came to live with me, I thought I felt secure, but the measure of personal safety I felt after her arrival increased exponentially in the cradle of her soft snoring. I knew she would give her life to protect me.

Rusti taught me the true meaning of "companion animal." Her love was unconditional, and she was a shining example of many of the virtues I'm still working on to claim as my own. My deep love and respect for her, the results I witnessed from the pet psychic who helped us early on, and my desire to pass the inspiring gift of an animal's love on to others opened a door for me.

And later on, when I cried out for guidance in finding a livelihood that would both inspire me and help others, these feelings and events created my vision for the future—the facilitation of the bond between humans and animals for the highest good of all concerned. ❀

3

Reading Masada

A beautiful big black, white, and silver-gray Akita, Masada was a dog who led the good life. Her human companions, my good friends Bruce and Patou (rhymes with "aah-choo!"), had adopted her when she was just a young pup, after having owned a couple of cats that died prematurely. They had become deeply attached to their young kitties, only to have them attract diseases that took them to the other side while they were still teenagers in pet years. The couple hoped that changing species would break their bad luck with pets.

Patou loved her gentle dog, but was sometimes afraid of her behavior. Athletic Patou took Masada out for a daily run, always wary, keeping an eye out for any other dogs that might cross their path, because while Masada was very friendly toward humans, she was not so friendly toward other dogs. And it wasn't just any other dog the sizable Akita exhibited aggressive behavior toward—it was little dogs. Patou jogged through the neighborhood, terrified that at any moment a small dog on the street would inspire Masada to take her on a wild, out-of-control leash ride.

Having practiced psychic counseling on humans for several years, and with months of focused study on animal communication behind me, I felt ready to try out the process on my first animal subject. So on a visit with Masada's human family in Southern California, I decided to test how the messages came through and see if the process was the same as it was with human clients.

Hugged by a luxurious armchair, relaxed and alone with Masada in my friends' peaceful living room, I asked the dog for her attention. I let her know I wanted to have a chat with her and that I'd like to talk to her through telepathic pictures. She already knew me and seemed quite open to the process, letting me know by stretching out into a relaxed position.

Why do you dislike small dogs? I asked.

It's not all dogs that make me feel aggressive, she told me. *Small, snappy dogs with big attitude problems make me want to put them in their place.*

Sending me telepathic pictures of tense small dogs on the defensive while they walked with their humans, Masada "showed" me it was her duty to protect her beloved Patou. Her pictures indicated that several small dogs had barked and acted aggressively first, causing her reaction.

She graphically showed me one case of a small dog that leaped out of a moving SUV and ran toward her while barking aggressively. Patou sprayed the small dog with pepper spray to stop it, basically saving its life (although the dog's human didn't see it that way).

Masada had once killed a small, aggressive neighborhood dog. The little dog lived right next door and barked at her continuously through the wrought iron fence separating the two backyards. Patou warned her neighbors that the small dog had been seen outside the fencing and that her Akita would not tolerate its presence in her own backyard should the dog get through. But her warnings went unheeded. The dog eventually did squeeze through the bars and Masada casually snapped its neck. Subsequently, Patou installed chicken wire around the perimeter of her yard.

Masada did not feel she was aggressive toward dogs that didn't have attitude problems, although she did consider herself an alpha dog who needed to establish the hierarchy by taking other dogs down. Her intense curiosity and lack of experience with other dogs also caused problems because her caretakers couldn't risk many encounters, even though at times all she wanted was a whiff. (Bruce and Patou did take the risk of introducing Masada to a friend's dog, who became very special to Masada. With concerned humans standing by, Masada established the hierarchy by pinning the other dog down—a natural dog-to-dog communiqué—after which the two canines became fast friends.

In seeking answers to the aggression dilemma, Patou had once consulted a knowledgeable veterinarian, who told her that one of the problems might be Masada's appearance. He said that the hair on her neck stuck out, making the towering dog appear to be in an aggressive mode at all times and triggering a defensive reaction in other dogs.

My first animal communication with Masada wasn't very long or elaborate. Being in my friends' comfortable home was the safest possible situation a beginner can choose.

That initial session moved me forward once I checked back in with Patou. The information fit with what she knew of the situation firsthand. Talking with Masada was a critical turning point, encouraging me to go on with animal communication. Not long afterward, another person asked me to help with his pet's behavioral problems.

Negotiating with my Higher Sources, I requested that they send me more pet psychic clients if I were meant to serve people and their beloved pets in this way. And the phone kept ringing. ☀

Section II

Quiet Conversations

*"Until one has loved an animal, a part of
one's soul remains unawakened."*

*~ Anatole France (1844 – 1924)
Author and Nobel Peace Prize winner*

Private clients with a variety of pet-related issues gave me a chance to practice using telepathy with animals. Before I went public and declared my new vocation, I met many animals and people who confirmed for me that psychic counseling and animal communication had a lot in common.

While my telepathic communication skills were honed, I knew very little about animal breeds, their common ailments, or behavioral problems. The private sessions that follow inspired and guided me with each success. ☀

4
The Unemployed Blue Heeler

Mandy, a woman in a wheelchair, came to see me at a benefit for an animal shelter in eastern Washington state. She would be the one to remind me that choosing a dog that matches the capabilities of his or her human companion is absolutely essential.

As Mandy's good friend Nadine helped her to the top of the stairs and into the room where I was working, I could see that Mandy was able to walk, although she was very unsteady. Accompanied by her young blue heeler, Blue, she was beside herself with worry once she spotted my 10-year-old chow, Rusti, lying calmly behind my chair.

Mandy and Nadine stopped in their tracks. They knew Blue's aggressive history with other dogs, and their caution proved accurate when he immediately attacked the calm chow. After removing Rusti to an adjoining room for her safety, the session was under way.

I didn't have to concentrate very hard as pictures of Blue's problems flooded in.

Mandy confided tearfully, "He runs so close to my wheelchair, I'm afraid I'll injure him. And he chases cars. He also nips at my heels when I'm standing and has accidentally knocked me down three times. I don't know what to do."

It was the classic case of a dog lover falling in love at an animal rescue center and making an emotional decision to take the dog home, even though the person's lifestyle and limitations make the breed completely unsuitable.

Blue's energy was scattered and confused. His small eyes darted from place to place in the room in search of a focus for his overflowing intensity. The feeling for me was one a human might have who has been bed-bound for months. Unexpressed energy like that in a dog turns into aggression, and Blue needed to run and run for hours. He also desperately needed a job.

The blue heeler, also called an Australian cattle dog, is a sturdy, compact canine, highly intelligent, and a great watchdog. The breed has a very strong herding instinct, which means it has a natural propensity to nip at anything near the height of a person's heels. With untrained cattle dogs, this can lead to serious consequences, like an attempt to herd young children into the house by nipping at the backs of their legs.

A heeler also needs intense daily exercise, something my client was unable to provide. For this breed, in particular, I'm not exaggerating when I say "intense" and "daily." Confined to the house for much of the day, Blue exhibited understandable aggression from pent-up frustration and lack of exercise.

Blue was too wound up and anxious to carry on much of a conversation, but I got his message loud and clear.

Animal shelter personnel and volunteers understand the importance of matching a breed with a person's capabilities, but good Samaritans often take on the care of a dog they can't handle with the best of intentions—like saving the animal from being euthanized. However, it almost never works out when the initial match is a bad one.

Sadly, I had to advise Mandy to consider a dog more suitable to her needs. Allowing Blue to go to a home where he had a chance to run and work was the best move for both of them because the dog was ready to explode. In fact, he already had, both during the session and at other times. Each time they ventured out, Blue's aggression toward other dogs was being directed more and more toward people.

Both women agreed that my advice was best. Meanwhile, Nadine volunteered to take the dog out running every day until they could find a better place for him to live.

*   *   *

An ideal adoption for Blue would have been to a ranch hand or a family looking for a dog to herd sheep or cattle. If his fate was to become a city-dwelling dog, he could also have been happy with a very athletic person who took him running, preferably more than once a day, or someone who enjoyed canine games like flyball or obstacle courses. Blue heelers are not unlike many very intelligent dogs who need both physical and mental stimulation, which dog sports provide. What heelers need at the end of the day is a feeling of happy exhaustion in order to sleep soundly and be psychologically balanced.

Mandy had been concerned for Blue's safety because he ran so close to her wheelchair when they went out for a walk. That's exactly how a herding dog works—up close and personal. Observe how any blue heeler herds a group of sheep or cattle by nipping at their hoofs and you'll see what I mean.

Mandy would have been much better off with a dog like a Sealyham terrier, a low-energy dog that makes a great cuddling companion. The Dog Breed Info Center (www.dogbreedinfo.com) describes Sealyhams as "low-energy couch potatoes," perfect for a person in a wheelchair who takes a daily moderate walk. ❀

Choose the Dog That's a Match Made in Heaven

A dog will be part of your family for an average of a dozen years, so choosing the right breed is an important decision. The American Kennel Club provides information to help you select the right dog for your particular household.

While general guidelines are helpful, there are also variations and exceptions to the rules. Here are some things to consider before taking home a new canine friend:

- *Exercise needs.* Active families might prefer high-energy dogs for jogging, hiking, and playing ball. More sedentary people might seek out quieter animals. Working dogs (like blue heelers) need lots of exercise and are rarely passive—agility trials, flyball games, and other activities suit them perfectly, and they make excellent pets when given a job to do.

- *Size.* Large dogs are not as well suited for elderly people, apartment dwellers, or mild-mannered handlers, although some large and energetic dogs can adapt to more cramped surroundings if exercised regularly. Small dogs may be a tripping hazard for the elderly or inappropriate for children, but may be perfect if you want a lap dog.

- *The dog's coat.* This may not be an obvious consideration, but long-haired and double-coated dogs shed like crazy, leaving tufts of hair that float about the house and can land in the most unsuitable places. Meticulous housekeepers will be happier with non-shedding breeds.
- *Training.* Breeds that are designed to work independently (like working breeds) require a firm hand when training; those that are easier to teach are breeds that work closely with their human companions. An older dog that's retired from service is a great companion for those less patient with the training process, but pups from a breed that's easier to train might be just as good. For the most part, hounds, terriers, and northern dogs are intelligent and independent, making them harder to train. Working dogs that pay close attention to commands tend to be golden retrievers, Labrador retrievers, border collies, German shepherds, and Shetland sheepdogs, to name a few.
- *Temperament.* Although there's wide latitude when it comes to temperament, general guidelines for different breeds do exist. For example, Akitas are thought of as tough, loyal, protective, aloof, dominant, aggressive to other animals, and often challenging. But many Akitas are just the opposite or have some of these characteristics and not others.
- *Other breed characteristics.* Hounds follow their eyes or noses and are sometimes oblivious to anything else around them, including their human companions. Dachshunds bond closely with their families, and greyhounds and whippets are sweet and gentle. Terriers are generally loud, tough, and independent, but Airedales are often somewhat protective and bond very closely to their humans.

5

Nervous Maxwell

Thirteen-year-old Maxwell was a beautifully blended black and white tuxedo cat with the physique of a chunky farmhouse cat who had enjoyed many hearty feasts. But his temperament was anything but that of a contented, lazy feline. Max was very nervous and fearful, and his caretaker, Beth, wanted to find out why.

I'm a cat without a country, he told me. *A second-class citizen.*

I could sense that he knew he was loved by his human but he did not feel like a part of the family. He conveyed that he lived in a house where other animals enjoyed a higher standing and where his safety and security were compromised.

I don't know if this is my permanent home, he said. *I could be devoured at any time or mutilated by one of the dogs who lives here. The only safe place is under the bed.* Beth confirmed that, indeed, Max spent most of his time there, but the information surprised her, as she had owned Max for more than a decade.

I suggested that Max be made to feel more a part of the family. He had showed me that he shared a food bowl with the other cats but he really wanted his own bowl, preferably with his name on it. He also craved soft food. Because the other cats could not manage soft food for dietary reasons, Max was required to eat hard food out of the community bowl.

Max sent this information to me telepathically by showing me a picture of the Fancy Feast® TV commercial where the beautiful cat has his own crystal dish of delectable chunky soft food. I felt not only a sense of the cat in the commercial being respected, valued, and cherished, but my mouth watered for the soft morsels. Max wanted some respect and some of that tasty-looking flaky tuna!

Additionally, Max wanted a place where he could feel safe from the dogs. He showed me that in the past, he had been traumatized by witnessing a chase ending in a neighbor cat being killed by a dog. Max did not trust any of the canine species, including the ones he lived with, even though they were gentle dogs.

As I continued to tune in to his energy, I also felt stuffed up and saw some runny eyes and congestion that felt like hay fever. Beth confirmed that Max had such a condition, including an upper respiratory infection that was being treated with antibiotics. I suggested a visit to the veterinarian for an allergy assessment.

But Max had experienced even more trauma. I felt my heart grow heavy as he relayed his grief to me. Beth validated this feeling, telling me that Max had been saddened by the death a few months earlier of his friend and fellow feline, Sumo, who had been his near-lifelong companion. I felt that Beth needed to grieve the loss of Sumo with Max, letting him know out loud that she also felt sad. I knew this process would help flush Max out, freeing up the respiratory congestion.

As far as the dog terror, I sent Max pictures of standing his ground, hissing, swiping the air, and, as a last resort, scratching a nose with his claw. My telepathic pictures showed him that most dogs ran the other way if they received a slight scratch on the nose. Beth said she knew this would work with her mild-mannered dogs because they avoided confrontations with kitty claws at all costs.

I also wanted Beth to create a place in her house that would be a refuge for Max: That meant a room where the dogs were not allowed or at least a very high scratch pole or bookcase where Max could retreat. Because the dogs roamed the house freely, Max always felt frightened.

My session with Beth and her willingness to follow through worked wonders for the sweet cat's confidence. She bought Max his very own bowl and painted his name right on it in big letters. Once that was done, he ate twice as much food and really enjoyed his own brand of dinner.

On a follow-up phone call, Beth reported that Max had come out of his funk beautifully and no longer seemed to be afraid of the dogs. The dogs also stopped chasing him, as they had been reacting to the cat's fear, and that fear had dissipated.

During another follow-up session, I conducted a body scan on Max, a process where I psychically "scan" the animal's body. Sensing a high level of tension, I located a big pocket of stress in his tail. It felt like an electrical live wire. I suggested that Beth pet Max in long strokes, from his head all the way down to the tip of his tail, while visualizing the stress and tension flowing out of his tail as she stroked it.

"He seemed to really enjoy that!" she later reported. "He's much more peaceful and loves the special attention of his own dish with the soft food in it. The upper respiratory infection has also cleared up. I've had Max in my life for 13 years, and this is the most together emotionally he's been with dogs around. Thanks so much for your help."

Max now felt at home, more confident, more loved, cherished, and respected. But several months later, Max needed my help again.

Beth had recently married, and Max overheard the new couple talking about relocating. Visions of spending three days in a cat carrier during the move made his thyroid malfunction. He quit eating and began to lose weight.

As I tuned in, I felt Max was determined to avoid the long trip. Understandably concerned, Beth sought the advice of her veterinarian and popped bitter-tasting pills down the poor boy's throat twice a day. Max grew thinner.

Beth wanted to know if he were making his transition to the afterlife, but I told her he planned to stay a bit longer. I also felt that Max's physical symptoms resulted from emotional upset and advised Beth to give Max a two-day break from medication. After that, I advised her to crush the pills up in some tuna, or dip them in a little butter to make them go down easier.

I also suggested that she allow Max to decide whether to continue with the medication. "If he refuses to eat the food with the pills in it, just allow him to make that choice," I counseled.

As a conscientious pet lover, Beth had carefully considered her animals prior to choosing her animal-loving husband and prior to buying a new home. Excited that the new place had lots of windows and perches for Max, she worked at relaying her enthusiasm about the move to her long-standing companion.

Beth had also carefully thought about the trip to their new home and how she could best make Max comfortable. She planned to have an open cat carrier where he could go in or out inside the car, and both of us sent those pictures to Max. I recommended that she talk to Max a bit more about the move, and gave her some tips on how to travel with him in greater comfort, but Max consistently sent me pictures of himself in spirit form in the new house, which I took as a strong indication that he wouldn't be making the three-day trip.

Only a week later Beth called to tell me that her veterinarian wanted to perform open-heart surgery on Max, but neither one of us felt that was a good option. Beth had promised Max that he would never have to spend time in the cat carrier again nor be forced to visit the vet.

After withdrawing the thyroid medication, Beth told me that Max perked up and went outside to enjoy the flowers. His behavior encouraged Beth, and both of us were satisfied that we'd made the right decision.

An emotional Beth called me the next day to say Max had made his transition just after she went to work. "He really didn't want to travel, did he?" she asked.

"No, he didn't. He was pretty clear about that, although he will be in your new home in spirit. His happy yard visits were his final rally before crossing over. Both pets and people often become more aware and lively, kind of like a last good-bye, before leaving their bodies," I told her.

Max had found a deep peace and lightness of being on the other side and had reconnected with his cat buddy, Sumo. He sent me images of the two of them watching bugs in some geraniums, and made me feel as if his physical exit made room for Beth to enjoy a new connection with a cat named Lydia.

*   *   *

Beth, accompanied by her toy poodle, Sam, was at the shelter to pick up Max's ashes when she noticed a little tortoise shell cat. I had told her that her next cat would choose her and that she would not be looking for a cat at the time. In an earlier session, her other cat, Alistair, had shown me that a youngster would be joining the family. Because Alistair was 13, his perception of a kitten included any young feline with a playful attitude.

Although the little cat at the animal shelter was stuck in a cage, her spirit was undeterred. A very affectionate and lively five-year-old, Lydia was biding her time waiting for Beth to find her there and take her home. When Sam the poodle approached the cage, Lydia pressed her whole body against the wiring and tried to play with him. Sam also became animated and frolicked around the outside of the cage as Lydia purred.

Not only was Lydia very chatty, but she was familiar with Beth, showing me pictures of a previous lifetime they'd had together as neighbors more than a hundred years before. She sent me the feeling that she had lived three houses down from Beth, who was a little girl. She said her encounter with Beth had taught her that animals could be more than just workers: They could also be beloved companions.

In that lifetime, Lydia was a working cat who caught barn mice, but she was never very close to her human family. The little cat got very different feelings from the neighbor girl— feelings of love and belonging. Lydia yearned to be an animal companion to someone like Beth but died young, her early demise related to a parasite carried by the vermin she was expected to control.

"So you're saying that we've been together in other lifetimes?" Beth asked.

"Not exactly together, but acquainted," I told her.

"Would you ask her if we've been together in this lifetime?"

"She says yes and there is a name coming through. It's Mini."

"Wow," said the stunned Beth. Then she told me the story of Mini.

Mini was a small cat to whom Beth had been very attached. It had been difficult to let Mini go, but when she passed on, the cat made room for Beth to welcome Max into her house as a rescue.

"Years ago, I went to the same animal shelter I visited yesterday," she said. "I was there to pick up Mini's ashes. I visited the cat cages and put my face close to the bars. When Max reached out through the bars and patted my face with his paw, I was hooked."

Mini's death had made a place for Max in Beth's home, and now Max was returning the favor. The two cats were connected in a circle of life that made their transitions easier on Beth and served the needs of each feline friend.

Beth decided to rename Lydia, calling her Hailey after the Idaho town she loved, and the cat sent me a feeling of being honored with such a loving name.

Every sense I had about Hailey was that she was willing to try new situations and places. Fearless Hailey was ready to take on her new people and pet friends and could hardly wait for Beth to come back and pick her up. She knew she had scored the old familiar home she'd waited for.

*   *   *

As a postscript to Max's story, it's important to note that sometimes pets with uncertain early lives can often be reassured very easily.

Riley, one of a pair of cats who had the good fortune to be rescued by Sue and her husband, Tom, was one such animal.

Sue contacted me because she was worried about Riley's behavior. At one and a half years old, the orange-striped cat was young in body and spirit but a nervous wreck. Not only were Sue and Tom planning a long vacation, they were also planning a move out of the only home he'd known, where a steady stream of potential buyers invaded the family's space. Wanting to protect her fragile and frightened cat, Sue put him in the car and in his carrier twice when strangers came to look at the home, unknowingly increasing Riley's anxiety.

Soon, the young cat began to act terrified of Sue, running out of the room when she came in, frightened of ending up in 'the box' again. He also jumped away erratically from his food in the middle of the meal, dashing away after taking only a bite.

The first message from Riley's celestial guides was, "Nothing good has ever happened to this cat involving either a car or a carrier."

Riley's temperament was completely opposite that of the laid-back, pure black Toby, his big adopted brother, who he relied on like a rock. Toby, who came into the family about eight months after Riley, was the calm, collected, midnight-black cat who acted like an anchor. He enjoyed Riley's antics, though he showed me that he classified some of the young cat's behavior as simply Riley's dramatic streak. Toby also showed me that he made himself immediately available when Riley was scared and needed to hide behind him.

Sue and I spent some time in our phone session, telepathically reassuring Riley about his place in the house, letting him know his position was safe for a lifetime, and assuring him that Sue would not put him in the carrier for now. I also thanked Toby, who piped up to say he would be happy to help and support in any way.

Sue called me about a week later to report that results had been almost instantaneous: The same evening we talked on the phone, Riley began eating normally. He was no longer spooked or terrified; in fact, he was calm.

"I don't know how you do it or what you did, but it worked," Sue said.

"I'm happy to be a facilitator of communication," I said, feeling a sense of gratitude to my Higher Sources, who had partnered with me to resolve Riley's anxiety. ☀

6

Magic Finds a Mate

In spring, a young rabbit's thoughts turn to love (even if he's been neutered), and that was the case for Magic, a pure white bunny who got his name because he looked like he'd been pulled out of a silk top hat. His human, Chantal, scheduled a session to ask me about his desires, and a bunny girlfriend was tops on his list.

Intuitively, I sensed that Magic led a life of luxury, where he was king of the castle. He had a wonderful toy-filled habitat that encompassed the entire large kitchen area, where knee-high fencing was set up so he could play safely and he had been trained to use a box full of cat litter.

Bunny life for Magic included high-quality food and a watchful, loving human caretaker—everything a bunny could want, short of a girlfriend. He also had a cat friend, Cyril, who was currently in the dog house, Magic told me, because of the cat's insistence on bringing headless rodent treats to Chantal through an open window at night.

Magic wanted to commune with another animal of his own variety, especially one of the opposite sex, and Chantal was eager to please him.

"Magic also wants to go with you when you shop for his new friend," I told her. "He says he'll show you which rabbit he's choosing."

"Do they allow that kind of thing?" Chantal asked me.

"Usually they do," I said. "Just take him with you, and when you've picked out a couple of female rabbits, put each of them with Magic in a grassy area and see what happens."

Chantal did just that, and the message was clear. Magic chose a jet-black bunny within just a few minutes of their meeting at the rabbit rescue center. The black and white rabbits reminded their new caretaker of bunny yin and yang as they became acquainted.

"I made an appointment with a woman who knew a lot

about rabbits," Chantal reported to me later. "She was already aware that Magic was cage-free and lived in my kitchen, and she told me about a special sweet and submissive black rabbit. While I made plans to visit Rabbit Rescue, the proprietor told me she would help with the introductions and see how it went."

The two women watched with amusement as they placed the two rabbits into a pen together. The black female bunny approached Magic and lay down. They looked comfortable together, and both women felt the rabbits recognized each other. Lola, the black bunny, rode home in the same carrier with Magic as more bonding took place and Magic shared his love of riding in the car with his new girlfriend. When she returned home, Chantal let the bunnies loose into their new kitchen habitat.

"Lola hopped everywhere and Magic followed right behind her," Chantal told me. "After a few days she became the boss, giving him orders. Lola adopted me right away, too, licking my ankles several times.

"Lola responded to her name almost immediately and even though Magic is a young macho male, his behavior became a little bit more reserved around her. It's very cute," Chantal noted. "Lola has started to gain a bit of weight due to the good food here. Magic is always close behind her, and they're never far from each other."

Chantal bought a thick rubber runner to cover the kitchen floor in order to give the rabbits more traction, then reported that they were "running through the kitchen like crazy."

Checking on the bunnies' progress after a few months, I learned that Chantal was experiencing a prolonged illness that forced her to find a new home for the bunny lovers: The doctor had diagnosed a stomach parasite that he told her was the result of keeping rabbits.

"I took them to a special place with lots of animals, asking the people there to try and find a home where they could stay together, and they did. I called a few times to check on them in their new home, and they were fine," she told me.

On my own I wanted to take a few minutes to check in telepathically on the bunny lovers. They were still happily together, living in a screened patio, and being well cared for by a human who, according to the feeling they sent me, adored them.

In scientific circles, the attribution of human emotions to

animals (anthropomorphism) has been taboo for many years, but researchers are finally beginning to acknowledge what people who love pets have always known: Animals have feelings. New scientific evidence supports what I find when tuning in to an animal: Their emotions seem to be very basic, but they include love, fear, jealousy, and grief. And so it was with Magic and Lola that when I checked on them in their new home, they sent me a profound feeling of gratitude and security, along with a picture of their new caretaker gazing down on them with love in her eyes.

In cases like Chantal's, in which she felt she had to relinquish her beloved bunnies, people often ask me if their animals are upset or angry. The opposite is true. Instead of imparting blame or regret, animals convey gratitude for what they've been given in their previous home. They easily let go of one set of circumstances for another, especially when both situations are equally favorable. Even when an animal is lost and adopted by a new family, he doesn't pine away for his old caretakers. What's left is the sense of love and appreciation for the previous set of circumstances and an easy adaptability to the new life—something that's not always easy to hear for a grieving person who has lost a pet.

In contrast, if by some chance an animal's living situation becomes intolerable, it will consider leaving, even if it means becoming feral. ☀

7

Daisy Mae and Dusty

Margaret had two small poodles: dark chocolate Daisy Mae and cream-colored Dusty. Both were six years old.

When Margaret adopted Daisy, the pup was three months old and very sick. Raised in a puppy mill, she had ear mites and ear infections that ultimately became a blood infection. Margaret wasn't sure whether Daisy would make it, but the care Daisy received couldn't have been more attentive. Her new loving "mom" held her constantly, wrapping her in sheets because of erupting boils all over her body. The little poodle recovered and, though scarred, was adored no less because of it.

The first year of her life, Daisy Mae loved riding in the car, going everywhere with Margaret. When the little dog was six months old, Margaret adopted Dusty. He loved riding in the car, too, and the two poodles got along well.

"The problem started about six months ago," a puzzled Margaret explained when she contacted me. "The three of us got in the car as usual. Daisy began yelping and jumping from the front seat to the back, over and over. She wouldn't stop, no matter what I did, so I turned around and returned home. Since then, she makes this high-pitched, shrill 'scream' and has sort of a panic attack whenever she knows she's going in the car. I have to put her in a carrier to take her to the groomer or the vet, and she yelps the whole way."

Margaret reported that once she and the dogs arrived at their destination, Daisy was as good as gold. But she wouldn't ride peacefully unless she was in Margaret's loving arms. When Margaret and her husband, Don, traveled together, Daisy was fine once she realized Margaret would hold her as Don drove.

"But she still yelps and cries when I drive because she can't get into my lap. Now Dusty has started to howl when Daisy cries. I have to take them to the groomer each month

41

and to the vet occasionally, and it's become a horrible chore."

Margaret had tried talking to Daisy, visualizing calmness and sending her mental pictures. Nothing had worked, so she called me as a last resort.

When I tuned in to the little dog, the feeling was one of being out of control. I felt as if the car had stopped suddenly, and I lurched forward. I felt no injury, only a loss of control.

I suggested administering a few drops of Rescue® Remedy (a product consisting of flower essences that often calms nervous dogs), sending Daisy green healing energy, and putting her in a secure carrier or a doggie seat belt.

These strategies helped momentarily, but Daisy would inevitably resume her distressed howling. Determined to keep working with Daisy, I received the message that each time she exhibited her out-of-control behavior, she should be taken back home. I instructed Margaret to tell Daisy why she was being left at home.

"Keep working with the Rescue® Remedy," I suggested. "Meanwhile, I'll continue to work from here, reassuring Daisy. I'll conduct a special session with her tomorrow to find out if there are any other reasons for her anxiety and what we can do about it."

Riding in the car reminds me of when I first came to live with this wonderful caretaker, Daisy told me the next day. *Several car trips early in my life ended up at the vet's, where it was painful, even though I knew they were trying to help me. The only thing that made it bearable was the warmth of my human mom's body and her calm reassurances when she held me close. So I associate the car with those warm feelings, the pain of the boils, treatments at the vet, and my being held.*

On three occasions, Margaret decided to take Dusty with her in the car and leave Daisy home.

"The first time I left Daisy home, she started whining as I was getting ready to leave," Margaret recounted. "I explained that only Dusty could go because riding in the car seemed too traumatic for her. She calmed down, but then when I called Dusty to go with me out the door, Daisy started yelping. I picked her up and placed her on her favorite chair, again telling her why she was staying home. She watched us leave with a sort of shocked look of disbelief but was totally quiet.

"The second time, Daisy yelped as we left, so I went back in the house and told her again why she had to stay. Again she became quiet. Same thing the third time," Margaret said.

I instructed Margaret to leave Daisy home three more times, and we'd go from there.

On the third trip, Margaret decided to try and take both dogs to the groomer.

"We were only down the street when Daisy started yelping, so I turned back home and brought her into the house. I took Dusty to the groomer, explained what was going on, then went back for Daisy. The people at the groomer's salon joined me in sending her peaceful green light. This time, Daisy didn't yelp in the car. She whined a little and kept trying to get in my lap, but because I drive a stick shift, I couldn't let her—I just held her on the seat with one hand as much as I could. She finally stayed and didn't cry."

When Margaret picked Dusty and Daisy up from the groomer, both dogs were quiet the entire drive home.

The groomer was another negative association with the car, Daisy told me.

They're nice to me there, but my skin is sensitive and some of the perfumes make me sneeze. I don't like getting a bath, and the sound of scissors makes me cringe, Daisy relayed.

*   *   *

I was pleased with the progress we were making, but I also knew we were not totally out of the woods. I encouraged Margaret to continue taking Daisy back home whenever she acted up in the car.

The next time Margaret phoned me, she reported a regression.

"I took Daisy and Dusty visiting friends yesterday," she began. "We got about a mile down the road when Daisy started her routine again, with Dusty joining in. I stopped the car and put Daisy in her carrier, but she only became louder. I told her I would take her back home if she kept yelping, which she did. So all of us went back to the house and I took Dusty alone. Daisy stayed in her chair as we left.

"Dusty loved being in the car without Daisy," Margaret continued. "Midway through my visit, I went back for Daisy. Happy to see me, she eagerly wiggled into the car. Although she whined a little and kept trying to get into my lap, we got there without a lot of noise. Both Dusty and Daisy were quiet and good on the way home."

43

In a subsequent conversation with Margaret several days later, I learned that Daisy had become grouchier than normal. She would trick Dusty, growl at him, and, if Daisy was sitting by Margaret first, wouldn't let Dusty come near. After a few days, Daisy would be nice to Dusty again for a while. But the cycle would repeat itself, and Daisy was becoming more intimidating.

"Dusty backs off when she gets like that," Margaret told me. "But I have to take Dusty's side sometimes so that I can pet him—then Daisy will move away and sit by herself. She is such a control freak for her age and size—I have to confess it's cute to watch, and sometimes I have to laugh."

Apparently, Daisy's jealously from being left home had resulted in some aggressive behavior against Dusty. I told Margaret one thing that was happening was that when Dusty arrived home from their journeys, he could not help but share pictures with Daisy. Some of those pictures involved how much fun he had riding in the car. And any mental pictures Margaret had about the events were also being relayed, which contributed to making Daisy jealous, controlling, and possessive.

"Don't let her get away with it or this aggression will accelerate and become harder to correct," I cautioned.

I also suggested that Margaret needed to be alert to opportunities to reward Daisy. "Private time with you could be a great reward. Maybe the two of you could take a walk after returning home in a quiet car," I suggested.

Margaret followed my advice and a more harmonious household resulted.

"I took Daisy for a walk—just me and her. She loved that. She and Dusty are also getting along better than they have for a while, playing and running around the house together," a relieved Margaret said.

More than a year later, I called Margaret to check up on the poodles. She had purchased another car that allowed her to confine the dogs in the back, where they had more room but were restricted from jumping over the seats. But Daisy still paced back and forth in the new car until the first time the car stopped and the engine was turned off. Margaret planned her trips with a first quick stop to get gas or run into a store briefly, which calmed Daisy. *I have immediate reassurance that my human mom is coming back,* she told me.

When she had time, Margaret also walked Daisy to calm

her before they went anywhere. If they took a long trip and stopped overnight, they'd still have to make an initial stop when Daisy became anxious. Margaret had tried giving Daisy motion sickness pills and tranquilizers on long trips, and the best remedy had been one-sixteenth of a tranquilizer. Once the car pulled out of town and onto the freeway, and after that first stop was accomplished, Daisy settled down.

Checking in on Daisy offered me new insights.

At first, I feel anxiety being separated from my human mom, who rides all the way in front of the car, Daisy relayed. *I still feel more secure in her lap when I'm in a moving car. But after she stops once, she always comes to the back of the car and reassures me. I feel more settled after that.*

Suzan is helping me to associate the hum of the car's engine with calmness and I'm starting to get into that feeling. The car has a lot of bad associations for me that I'm trying to change but trips to the groomer and the vet are intermittent, so I never know whether the car trip will be good or bad.

*   *   *

The story of these two poodles doesn't end exactly how everyone had hoped. Let's face it, dogs have traumas they can't always overcome. No matter how much we talk to them about it, or want it to be different, not all dogs like riding in cars. But since buying her new car, Margaret is able to take both dogs along when she goes out, and the shrill "scream" from Daisy has turned to a whine that ends after the first stop. For Margaret, that's something she can live with.

What Margaret wanted when she called me was to have both of her dogs accompany her when she went on errands in the car, and eventually she got her wish. But opening her mind to the possibility that Daisy Mae might never be happy in the car was important. Unlike some people who contact me, Margaret was willing to consider adjusting to the unique needs of her pet. Others who can't accept an answer that doesn't fit their desires fight an uphill battle in which both pet and human continue to struggle disharmoniously. ☀

Taking the Chaos of Out of Car Rides

The following steps can benefit many animals who are afraid of riding in the car. These steps take time, but our pets are complex creatures and training them often requires as much patience as raising children.

- Get into a calm state and clear your mind of pictures that show your animal being upset and acting out.

- Administer a few drops of Rescue® Remedy, lavender oil, or another calming essence to the exterior of your animal's ears or on their gums.

- Escort your animal into the car, leaving the car turned off. Pet and soothe the animal until it has achieved a calm or sleepy state.

- Don't drive anywhere until you've practiced the prior steps successfully several times.

- Drive the car back and forth in the driveway or in front of your house until the animal is calm. Repeat this three or four times in one day, and then try to move forward the next day. Your animal will let you know when he or she is ready to move forward to the next step. If not, go back to step one.

- Drive a few blocks. Stay in tune with your animal's behavior and monitor the amount of time it takes before your pet settles down. When this has been reduced to 30 seconds or so, try moving on to the next step.

- Do an errand where you actually get out of the car for a very short stop.

- Drive onto the freeway *and* run an errand where you get out of the car for a longer period of time.

- Many car-fearing animals benefit from having the windows of the vehicle obscured. Tape black construction paper to the inside of the car windows and between humans and animals if possible. As a reward for calm behavior, remove one piece of paper between the animal and the people in the car or to reveal the outside landscape. If anxiety accelerates, replace the paper shield. Repeat the removal process when the animal becomes calm again.

- Reward your pet throughout the training process using treats and/or praise (some pets aren't motivated by treats). Remember to reward calm behavior, like by giving affection to a sleepy pet.

8

Gemma Adjusts

Robert's story is very common among people who adopt a cat from a shelter. Contacting me through my Web site (www.telepathictalk.com), he relayed a problem with his newly adopted cat, Gemma. The anxious kitty was peeing on the bed, one of the most common problems I deal with.

As I tuned in to the household, I clearly "saw" Robert sleeping with a woman I assumed was his wife or significant other, but the vision became fuzzy when I tried to get a picture of which side of the bed Gemma was using. In my vision, the location, a significant part of the imagery, moved between "Dad's" side of the bed and "Mom's," confusing me. I wondered if Gemma were targeting one of them specifically, which is normally the case. So I asked Robert to clarify the location.

"It's happening right in the middle of the bed, between where the two of us sleep," he said.

Robert's reply told me that Gemma was attempting to communicate to both of her human companions.

As I opened my heart and mind to connect with Gemma, my vision showed that she spent much of her time hiding out. Insecure in her new surroundings, Gemma shared that several other cats in her new home did not accept her as part of their pack. This was understandable, in light of the fact that neither Gemma nor her new family was really sure she had found a permanent home.

Robert expressed how much he admired Gemma's beauty and that he was committed to giving her as much time as she needed to integrate into the household. Yet the words he said and the feelings of his heart were disparate. The exotic-looking cat knew before I did that Robert's commitment wavered. Early on, I offered Robert tips on how to send Gemma messages of reassurance, which she had a hard time believing, making this case more difficult.

Along with an overwhelming urge to go outside, Gemma

conveyed that she had once happily experienced grass, trees, bugs, and flies. A high-energy kitty, she still loved and remembered the outdoors, but her new life was one where the cats stayed inside at all times. The other cats accepted that reality and had settled in, but Gemma craved the outdoors and was still adjusting to new rules, new people, and new animal companions.

Is the message about urinating on the bed related to wanting to go outside? I asked her.

No, she answered.

Is it about the kind of litter? I sent her numerous pictures of litter boxes and what she should be doing with them. I asked her how the litter felt under her feet, if she might prefer soft, sandy litter versus granular, and several other questions related to her bathroom habits.

It has nothing to do with the litter or the litter boxes, she told me.

What kept nagging me was a strong feeling of insecurity. *Are you feeling threatened with being taken back to the shelter?* I asked.

Yes. My dad is patient with me, but my mom wants to send me back. The cats here are mad because I'm making Dad clean up all the time. Snowball is hostile, Gemma added.

I shared this information with Robert, who confirmed that one cat in particular didn't like Gemma much—Snowball.

Gemma had other problems, too. Whenever the front door was opened, she darted outside. This concerned Robert because he often spotted dead cats on the side of the road in his neighborhood and feared that Gemma's bolting would attract a similar fate.

Gemma needed to understand the danger of running outside. I recommended that Robert picture in his mind what would happen if she were hit by a car. With this visualization technique, I asked him to follow that mental picture with one of Gemma staying in the house when he opened the door, and feeling safe, loved, and secure. Next, he was to repeat these two visualizations back to back. I also suggested that he tell Gemma out loud why he worried when she went out, knowing the pictures in his mind would follow his words.

"When she does it right, don't forget to thank and praise her for not hanging out at the door," I said. Gemma was already getting part of this message.

I asked Gemma if she understood why Robert wanted her

to stay indoors.

Yes, she said. *He shows me the pictures of the cats who get run over by cars. But I need to get out sometimes. I just can't be indoors all the time, cooped up with cats who don't like me.*

Because Robert really wanted Gemma to be happy, he asked me more than once if it would be better to return her to the shelter where someone who would allow her to go outside could adopt her. As Robert's anxiety rose, his resolve to give Gemma as much time as she needed to adjust to being an indoor cat faltered.

A few days after our initial session, I followed up with Robert, asking if there had been any new incidents.

"Yes, unfortunately, after three days of no accidents, the last two evenings Gemma peed on the bed. On my side, both times!" he said. "But the good news is that she seems more open to attention and has even come to sit with me twice. Plus, she sat on the couch with my girlfriend for the first time!"

The two of us sent her more reassuring messages. Robert asked me to transmit to Gemma that he and his girlfriend intended to keep her and weren't mad, just sad that she felt so upset.

Gemma was trying to claim Robert as her human by marking his side of the bed. I suggested that the next time Gemma peed on the bed, Robert should tell her that, although she was loved, kitties who peed in the house couldn't have the full run of the house.

"Give her a time-out in a carrier in a small utility room or in the garage. What we're shooting for is a consequence for her behavior," I said. "Start with a 10-minute time-out and increase it to 15 minutes if the behavior happens again. Tell Gemma she must use the litter box for your house to be in harmony."

"I'm willing to do the consequence, but I'm a little confused," Robert said. "She wants out of the house very badly, including into the garage, so I'm not sure how that works as a consequence."

"Make your time-out space one that's a definite consequence for her. You don't want to put her in a room full of toys, treats, and food. It should be somewhat small and sparse, and reserved for behaviors you can't tolerate," I advised. I also encouraged Robert to have any urinary tract infection or physical problems ruled out before giving Gemma the time-out.

Robert, a very conscientious caretaker, e-mailed me the same day to say he'd made an appointment with the vet. I offered a few pointers on getting a urine sample, which was sure to be a challenge.

"It was a traumatic night trying to get a urine sample," he wrote. "The vet gave me some special litter that doesn't absorb liquid. Gemma apparently didn't like it because she kept going into the box and coming out without doing anything. About five o'clock this morning, after she'd held it for over 10 hours, she finally climbed onto the pet bed she'd been sleeping on and squatted. I slid the plate under her backside and she peed right on it. I took the urine sample to the vet first thing this morning. Everything tested normal."

Although Robert did a great job of getting a urine sample under difficult circumstances, I urged him not to allow Gemma to pee in or near the pet bed. I suggested he lift her up and put her in the litter box when he saw her squat and to praise her like crazy when she went in the box.

The next time I spoke to Robert, Gemma was better, but there were still times when she urinated on the bed. After a short chat, it was easy to see that part of the problem was Robert's internal conflict. When someone is comfortable giving animals affection but conflicted about discipline, they often send telepathic pictures of the pet engaging in the wrong behavior. Meanwhile, the animal receives the communication that they're doing exactly the right thing. Telepathic pictures always override verbal commands.

Robert told me he had reconsidered using the consequence technique while continuing to allow Gemma to pee on the bed.

"If she's just peeing because she's stressed and insecure, I'm not sure punishment would help," he said. "What do you think of us just riding it out for a while and letting her settle in some more? We have plastic under the comforter on the bed and I can live with washing the plastic and comforter every day for now."

I knew allowing Gemma to use Robert's bed as a litter box would confuse the cat and ingrain the behavior and I explained that to Robert. I also offered a few more pointers that included closing the bedroom door and allowing access only to the litter box room in combination with catching Gemma in the box and offering lots of praise.

I suggested that Robert reward Gemma with anything she liked (including a bit of tuna) when she went in the litter box, and also gave him a tip about how to engage the other household cats in the process: "Give all the kitties a treat when Gemma does the right thing." I knew that if everyone got rewarded when Gemma went in the box, the other cats would make it their business to help train her.

Robert followed my advice, and doing so moved the process forward. But Gemma still wasn't cured in a single week. In her mind, the correct place to relieve herself was outside, which remained off-limits. And Robert's ambiguity was confusing to her.

After Robert spoke with Gemma twice, one evening she jumped onto the bed, sniffed at the plastic covering, then jumped down, went into the bathroom, and squatted on the rug. This made Robert feel depressed and defeated.

"I don't think she likes it here," Robert e-mailed. "I feel guilty and I'm reconsidering taking her back to the shelter so she can be with a family that will let her go outside."

Although I too felt the cat's ideal home would be one where she could go outdoors, I wasn't ready to give up. Knowing her fate was uncertain if she were returned to the shelter, Robert wasn't quite ready to give up either, so I asked him to at least give a time-out a try.

"She's not getting the message that peeing on the bed can't be tolerated," I explained. "Examine what you do now when she goes on the bed. Do you take her over there and tell her no, then show her the box again and reinforce that she's supposed to go in it?"

The notion of disciplining Gemma made Robert distraught, and his commitment to her fluctuated daily. When he said he'd do anything to integrate this young cat into his household, he meant anything but discipline, and that's very common with tender-hearted people.

I received an e-mail from Robert a week later that was the perfect illustration of the power of direct communication that people sometimes resort to when there's nothing left to lose.

"I just wanted you to know it's been six days in a row with no accidents," he began. "Gemma has started taking part in our daily play. She also sleeps on the bed with us most nights now.

"I had decided to give her the consequence of being confined whenever she peed on the bed, but it never came to that. Last Saturday morning she squatted on the bed in front of me. I picked her up before she released anything and put her into the litter box, telling her she had to go in there if she wanted the run of the house. We've had perfect litter box behavior ever since."

Our sessions encouraged Robert to talk to Gemma in a more deliberate way to get across a specific message. He told her if she peed outside the litter box, he would take that as a sign that she wanted to be taken back to the adoption center. He also told her if she didn't pee outside the box, he would take that as a sign that she wanted to live with him and his girlfriend. He reassured Gemma that he and his girlfriend really wanted her and hoped she'd choose to stay. Robert also wrote that he'd been holding back on how much he petted and kissed Gemma. Because he now felt he had nothing to lose, he started stroking her more and talking to her.

"If she's sleeping somewhere in the open, I come over and lavish attention on her. I also ask her to purr, and now she usually does. I love it!"

*　　*　　*

A cat often communicates or shows its insecurity by urinating on one person's side of the bed. When that happens, the cat is trying to say it feels afraid of, threatened by, or concerned about the person who sleeps on that side of the bed. I've frequently seen this behavior when someone reluctantly tolerates the cat as part of the household because it belongs to a husband, wife, or significant other. But there can also be an opposite reason for this behavior: Cats also use it to communicate that they love their new human and want to claim him or her as their own. This kind of message can also be meant to alert people to impending illness, situational stress, or some kind of concern for a member of the household.

One session of my talking with a pet can yield astonishing results, but normally, no amount of talking to a pet will change unwanted behavior if an animal's caretaker doesn't do his part.

Enlightened parents know that children need discipline and guidance in order to grow up as balanced human beings. Discipline is love, and reasonable discipline offered in a caring way is also essential for training pets. Many people don't understand that or can't quite implement the correct procedures, and the consequences are deadly: animals returned to shelters or euthanized for easily corrected behavior.

In Gemma's case, adjusting to a new home took a few months, and Robert was a real trooper. Diligent collaboration between animal communicator and caretaker finally paid off, providing Gemma with a permanent home where both the human residents and their pets found contentment.

*   *   *

The causes of Crystal's problems with the litter box were different. Mackenzie, her human caretaker, was trying everything she knew to resolve the problem, including using different kinds of litter.

The first time we checked in on Crystal, I felt she had a bladder infection, which was confirmed by a veterinarian and cured by antibiotics. Litter box problems were resolved for several months. But Mackenzie was understandably frustrated when Crystal began to go outside the box once again.

"I'm using silica gel litter right now," Mackenzie told me.

"Crystal seems to like that fine but says there's another kind she used to use that she liked better," I relayed. "It's the sandy, clumping kind."

"I hate that," Mackenzie said. "I've used it before but it's messy and we live in a small space."

"Would you consider using it if you put the litter box in the bathtub?" I asked.

"I put my body in there at least six times a week so the thought doesn't appeal to me," Mackenzie said.

I tuned in to Crystal again to continue the negotiation.

"Crystal says there's another litter box with another kind of litter she doesn't use," I told Mackenzie.

"That's right," Mackenzie confirmed. "It's made of corn."

"She's allergic to it," I said. "Corn is also the reason she has problems getting to the box on time: It's in her food and she's also allergic to ingesting it. The very first thing to do is to change her diet to a higher quality food. Can you do that today?"

Mackenzie said she could and immediately switched Crystal to a much better food she already had in the cupboard.

Just like people, animals respond to allergens like pollen, dust, food ingredients, household chemicals, and insect bites, to name a few. Their allergies can result in itchy or swollen skin, difficulty breathing, diarrhea, or vomiting.

Crystal had been vomiting profusely and also had runny stools. Three days later, the results were conclusive and undeniable. Crystal was making it to the litter box every time. Her digestive problems were gone and problems with elimination were cured. Our half-hour session and a change in litter and food cured her of months of litter box and nausea problems. ☀

Litter Box Issues

Not using the litter box is one of the most common reasons people call me for help with their kitties. There are lots of factors that contribute to this behavior:

- The cat is used to going outdoors and is adjusting to the use of a litter box.

- The "feel" of the kitty litter is unpleasant. Some cats prefer clumping litter; some prefer gravel-like litter (see box next page).

- The box needs to be cleaned out. Many, many cats are fastidious—in their ideal world, their caretakers would supply one box per cat, cleaned out twice daily.

- The litter box has another cat's scent. In many cases, cats are fine sharing a box, but if you're having a problem, this is something you can address easily.

- The cat is peeing on something new to make it "smell right." This is often the case when that item is a rubber-backed bathroom rug. Hubby dripping on the rug in front of the toilet can also be a trigger indicating it's okay to go there.

- The cat is upset at a person who doesn't want it around.

- The cat is trying to "claim" the human on whose side of the bed it's peeing. This is especially true of cats that have been shuffled from home to home or are newcomers to a home (especially where there are other cats already living there).

- Other cats in the house terrorize them while they're trying to go in the box.

- There are no consequences for the undesirable behavior. (Yelling is of no consequence to cats).

Litter Choices

There are at least six kinds of cat litter on the market right now, and most likely more to come. Every cat has a preference, which is where an animal communicator comes in when you're having litter box problems.

- *Traditional clay.* Some brands are scented, some are not, some are dust free.

- *Clumping clay.* Clumps can be scooped out, making odor control easier. Some brands are scented, many are neither flushable nor biodegradable.

- *Clumping non-clay.* This kind of litter is usually made from ground corn, wheat, sawdust, or plant material. It is usually flushable, less dusty, environmentally friendly, and pretty good at controlling odor, but be careful of mold.

- *Silica gel.* Great for absorbing moisture, flushable and long-lasting, but don't use this litter if your cat has respiratory problems.

- *Pellets.* Made from recycled newspapers, it is very absorbent, burnable, flushable, biodegradable, and environmentally friendly. But it's not very good at odor control.

- *Self-washing (a complete litter box system).* Fairly expensive, it works by water circulating over permanent granules and automatically dissolving cat feces and flushing them, along with urine, down the drain. A cleaning solution is automatically sprayed on the granules and a built-in dryer blows hot air to dry the granules out. It's environmentally friendly in the sense that nothing goes to the landfill, but remember to use all chemical solutions with caution.

9

Blossom and Marty

Blossom was a cute, perky little beagle who had some problems with jumping on the sofa and insistently licking her caretaker's face. Even when Angie tried to discourage her excited companion, the beagle's behavior persisted as he jumped at her face repeatedly.

When I tuned into little Blossom, I could feel her excitement about getting close to Angie's face. From Blossom's point of view, this was the beautiful place where loving words came from, and the little beagle felt an overwhelming affection toward this particular part of her human companion's body.

Many dogs like to smell a person's breath as a signature of their special person, and Blossom was no exception. But the literal "in your face" kind of attention Angie got whenever she sat down on the couch to relax had become a bit much.

I suggested that Angie sit with Blossom on the floor, close to the dog with her face and breath, to make the dog's compulsion a bit more manageable for both of them.

By our second phone session, Angie had spent some time on the floor with the beagle and reported that Blossom had become much less intense. To me, Blossom's feeling was one of satiation: What had been out of reach was now offered freely and she was less obsessed with making contact with Angie's face. When Angie gently guided her off the couch, Blossom complied right away without insistently coming back for more.

Angie also had a more difficult problem with Blossom that she needed to resolve: Blossom's tendency to eat other dogs' waste when out on a neighborhood walk. This behavior I knew would be harder to change, and I needed Angie's help. It's one thing to communicate what you want an animal to do or not to do, but it's another thing altogether to re-train the dog to leave compulsive behaviors behind.

After "showing" Blossom the unwanted behavior and communicating with her about how she could please Angie by refraining from that behavior, I instructed Angie to take some treats in her pocket out on their next walk and when they came upon some dog waste to pull Blossom away, gently say "No," and then offer her a treat.

At our follow-up session, Angie reported that Blossom seemed to understand the connection between the treats and the dog waste, but she was still unsatisfied with the results so far. Further questioning revealed that instead of following the suggested training plan, Angie had been avoiding the areas where she thought the dog waste would be. At the sight of dog waste, Blossom was given a treat. She knew there was a connection but she was confused about correct behavior.

I instructed Angie to take Blossom directly to those areas where she would normally eat the waste, allow her a quick whiff, say "No" calmly, and pull her away on the leash while simultaneously offering her a treat and saying "Good girl."

Angie followed these guidelines and Blossom then made the correct connection.

During this period I read in Beatrice Lydecker's book, *What The Animals Tell Me*, that eating animal waste (and gravel) often indicates a lack of HCL (hydrochloric acid) in the diet. Lydecker writes that animals seek out enzymes in animal waste that are normally found in HCL and used for breaking down proteins. Without HCL, these proteins ferment in the intestinal tract, producing uncomfortable amounts of gas soon after eating.

HCL tablets can be purchased from any health food store, and Lydecker recommends giving the pet one HCL tablet about 10 to 15 minutes before each meal, crumbling the tablet onto dry food and removing any water until after the meal (water dilutes the tablet and makes it ineffective).

Problems with dogs eating waste can also be about a need for more nutritional food. When low quality food is digested, it comes out smelling almost exactly like it did when it went in. A higher quality diet can often help with this problem, and some trainers suggest giving dogs, especially those that will eat anything, foods like pineapple that make the stool less appealing.

A few weeks later, Angie reported that all of Blossom's annoying behaviors had greatly improved, and she promised to search out HCL tablets at the store to resolve the lingering problem of waste consumption.

Angie wasn't very impressed with our first session. She felt that I had given her too much homework and had hoped I would just relay what she wanted to her pooch and the little beagle would comply. But as with many cases where certain behaviors have gone on for a long time, a half-hour talk proved inadequate.

Animal communication often takes at least two sessions. A psychic can read what an animal feels and how he or she reacts to certain smells or situations, and in most cases offer a remedy. But accomplishing behavioral changes usually requires the caretaker's help and cooperation in re-training, and change does not always happen right away.

*   *   *

A couple of sessions were also needed to resolve a different kind of eating disorder with Marty, a Japanese chin named after the comic Marty Feldman because of his big brown eyes.

The little black and white dog's human companion, Linda, loved him very much, and called one night to ask me if I could find out why he had suddenly stopped eating his dinner.

When I tuned in to Marty, I felt a tickle and a sensation around my nose, and quickly got the message that Marty didn't like the way his food smelled. And being no lover myself of the pungent spice, I lost my own appetite when I smelled garlic.

Linda confirmed that she had recently begun adding garlic to Marty's food after reading of its many benefits for canines. She told me she was actually trying to prime him by giving him some sliced turkey by hand, then setting his regular food down on the floor, with the garlic in it, for him to eat. But Marty thought it was stinky and unappealing.

I translated to him that Linda's main concern was for his health, which he understood, and he agreed to a compromise. Marty let me know in feelings and smells that he didn't mind the flaxseed oil Linda had also added to his food—it was no problem at all if she would agree to put that on the turkey. But he couldn't stomach the garlic.

At first Linda still wasn't clear on what Marty was willing to do. After giving him the turkey separately, she put his dog dish, still laden with garlic, back down on the floor. Marty wouldn't touch the stuff.

In a follow-up session, I explained again to Linda that Marty was not going to eat anything with garlic, and she finally stopped putting it on his food. Marty ate heartily, a grateful dog because his food once again smelled appetizing.

Marty was a smart dog, communicating clearly about the food during our first conversation. Another part of that communication was about his habitual scratching, which I told him annoyed Linda.

Immediately following that session, he would raise his leg toward his ear to scratch, then stop and look at Linda.

"I can actually see him thinking about it and putting his leg back down, knowing now that the behavior irritates me," Linda told me.

Following the two phone sessions, Linda reported that she felt much closer to her pooch once we had communicated, and thought he was ever so clever for having understood the telepathic messages I sent him. ☀

10

Necessary Losses

Late at night and long past office hours, a crisis call interrupted my calm evening.

Cheryl was having a hard time getting her emotions under control as the loss of Suzie, her 13-year-old cat, seemed inevitable. As a kinesiologist, Cheryl had done some testing to check on the cat's health. On Monday, the percentage of life force in Suzie's body was at about 85 percent. By Tuesday, it had gone down to 65 percent, and by the time she called me on Wednesday, the cat's vital signs were weak as Suzie ebbed away—Cheryl was measuring her life force at 45 percent.

"My cat's life force is quickly leaving her body," Cheryl said in a broken voice. She wanted to know how long she had left with Suzie, and if there were anything else she could do either to save her beloved feline or to help with her transition.

After sending me Suzie's picture in an e-mail, Cheryl called to hear what I had picked up on the cat's soul level.

Suzie's kitty guides immediately showed me pictures of the liberation she was anticipating from her ailing body: play with a butterfly in the garden. Suzie let me know that she couldn't do that any longer. But she showed me that, indeed, Cheryl could still do one more thing for her.

I can't groom myself, and I hate being dirty, she told me. *Could you ask my mom to keep me clean?*

I had run into that dilemma with cats before. On several occasions, a dying cat had told me it favored being euthanized once it had lost its ability to keep clean. That was Suzie's final request of her caring person—to keep her clean while she was still in her physical body.

The telepathic pictures the cat's soul showed me were of glowing internal organs and light switches being turned off within each of them. I relayed to Cheryl that I felt this message indicated organs were shutting down. She confirmed that message, saying she thought Suzie's kidneys had already stopped functioning and that other organs were quitting.

I sensed the cat wanted to pass on naturally and that she was in no real pain, a great relief to Cheryl. Suzie also let me know that Cheryl had taken wonderful care of her, that they'd had a great life together, and that Cheryl had done some healing work on Suzie to make her passing easier. Cheryl confirmed that she had performed several healing sessions on the lucky kitty.

Still, none of this information or confirmation made letting go easier for Cheryl, who sobbed throughout the session.

I really felt for her, remembering how I had euthanized my pet kitty, Batgirl, just a few years before. Bat's kidneys had also shut down, and she spent her last days drinking and urinating dozens of times a day. I could barely keep up with the litter box changes.

"How long do you think it'll be?" Cheryl asked just before our session ended.

"Just a few days, but I wouldn't be surprised if it's tonight or in the morning," I told her gently. "Please know that Suzie sends you an enormous amount of love and gratitude for all you've given her and that she won't be far from you even after she passes over. She's showing me that you will know she is near when you feel little depressions on the bed, like a cat walking around. While there'll be no physical kitty, you'll know she's there."

The next day, Cheryl called me to say she had been taking Suzie outside to enjoy nature for a few hours each day. Uncertain whether the cat preferred being indoors or out, she continued to be concerned as to whether she were doing the right thing.

"Suzie seems to be enjoying the times you take her outside and the coziness of being indoors as well," I told Cheryl. "She says you have the mix down perfectly. Hang in there, my friend. She's very comfortable with all you have done for her and all you are still doing."

"I do so appreciate your support in this very hard time for me and Suzie," Cheryl said. "Knowing that I'm doing the right things for her is very comforting. It's so hard to see her so weak and sick. I know she'll be happy and active again once she passes. Thank you so very much for your concern and many, many blessings for your continued service to grieving humans and our pets."

Suzie made her transition six hours later, while Cheryl slept. I saw her playing hide and seek in a field full of blooming daisies filled with a rainbow array of butterflies.

*   *   *

Tammy was another person who dearly loved her cat, Frazzle, and did everything she could to make her pet's passing easier.

Frazzle had led a charmed life with Tammy, who made sure Frazzle had the best food, water, toys, playful stimulation, kitty condo window seats, and medical care. But when Tammy contacted me, Frazzle was preparing to leave a body that was losing its ability to function.

As I scanned Frazzle telepathically, my focus stopped in her head area almost as soon I had begun the process. There was density and blockage, and something that looked like a small growth or tumor causing sensitivity.

"It's not in the sinus," I relayed to Tammy, "but appears to be on the right side near her ear as I look out of Frazzle's eyes. There's a ringing in her ears, some head congestion, and throat constriction. I feel numbness resulting from that constriction, as her body feels lighter and detached from the neck down. There's throbbing pain in the tail, especially the last third of it. While the pain is annoying, it's bearable and not sharp."

"What can I do to help?" Tammy asked me.

"Use your thumbs to rub behind her ears—no scratching please, only light rubbing," I told her. "She's also asking for light rubbing on her shoulders with your thumbs, but only for short periods of time. She requests a few drops of cream, canned tuna water, and meaty baby food.

"There are hard round objects in the back of her body that could be kidney stones, and she has to make an extra effort eliminating due to soreness like hemorrhoids. She says she needs extra warmth because she has a few chills.

"She wants help with passing as soon as she is unable to clean herself. She asks you to wash her for a few days while you say your good-byes, then please euthanize.

"The other cats in your home are also communicating with me. They're already aware of Frazzle's impending transition, so they're telling me it's not necessary for them to see her body once she's gone," I explained to Tammy. "Some pets wonder where their friends go when they are whisked away to the vet never to be seen again, but you have kept them all well informed."

I continued:

"Frazzle shows me that she's lounging in a sunny spot. I asked if she'd enjoy a heating pad, but she declined, feeling all tingly and anxious about the electricity going through the pad.

"She still enjoys some visual stimulation, like feathery toys, but is not in much of a playing mood most of the time. She also enjoys the visuals of birds outside the window, and shows me a wooly pad near a place that's warm where she can see outside.

"Frazzle wants you to know that she is aware of her special home and surroundings," I went on. "I can't remember if she was a rescued cat, but she says she once lived in a place that was cold—The floor was cold and I sense it was in a garage or like she spent times outside where there was not much warmth. She feels lucky because her life could have turned out much differently, and she knows she found a special human who knows all about cats.

"Frazzle has also enjoyed the other cats in your household, and shows me a younger one that she used to allow to pounce on her. The feeling is one of tolerance for that kind of play, but she is no longer as tolerant of the pouncing, although she did enjoy the game in the past. She can't play it now due to neck soreness. I saw a bony spine, and asked if she had lost weight. She said yes."

I ended the session by telling Tammy, "Frazzle sends you a profound and deep love and gratitude for a wonderful life. Please know that my heart is with you as you move through this difficult time."

Tammy wrote me a few days later:

"Frazzle was euthanized Monday night at home. She was glad to get out of her old and failing 18-year-old body. She was peaceful and ready to go. We had a very good life together; she was my welcoming committee, chatty cat, and queen of cuddling, all rolled into one cat.

"The other cats were very good to her these last few very tough days. It really is so different around here without her. I will miss her so much."

*   *   *

My session with Frazzle helped Tammy prepare for her

passing, but sometimes our animal companions move on unexpectedly.

I met Sophia, a small, older dachshund, when her caretaker, Olivia, requested a session about the little dog's increasing lack of bowel control. Olivia told me that Sophia was healthy other than her problem with incontinence.

Olivia lived in a beautiful old farmhouse that she and her husband had fallen in love with. They furnished it with lovely antiques and raised a family there. But her husband had passed away a few years before, the children were scattered across the country with their own families, and Olivia was planning to downsize. Just outside her bedroom window, construction on the foundation of a smaller modular home was taking place on adjacent property she owned.

A young couple who reminded Olivia of herself and her husband in the early years of their marriage had also fallen in love with Olivia's farmhouse. They had made an offer, Olivia had accepted, and escrow was expected to close within the month.

"Sophia climbs on my lap with a little help, but there's nothing wrong with her," Olivia told me. "I was raised to believe that she's 'just a dog,' but we've been together for more than 10 years now and I see her more as a beloved family member.

"I care deeply about her," Olivia added. "I just don't want the new carpets immediately ruined in the new house."

When I communicated her concern to Sophia, the little dog showed me in pictures that soiling the rugs wouldn't be an issue.

I see and hear the construction going on and I know about the planned move. I am looking inside the house but I don't go in. I see inside the windows but I am in my spirit body, she showed me.

How much longer will you be in your present body? I asked her.

About a month, she said.

Olivia was startled at the news. But only six weeks later I heard from her again.

"Sophia crossed over on Friday, the day my new house arrived!" Olivia told me. "She developed a cough that was cardio-related. I miss her so, but she's buried right off the bedroom deck of my new house and I feel that she's close. She was right. Her problem was never an issue in the new house."

*   *   *

Pets who have already passed on are also often a concern to people who deeply love their animals.

Sadie was one such person who called me for a phone appointment. She wanted to find out more about the death of her dog, China. Sadie felt better when the soul of the little Yorkie showed me some of his mannerisms and funny personality, making Sadie feel that China was fine on the other side. Both Sadie and I also knew the little dog was still around in spirit.

China helped me see where he used to sleep on the bed, which I relayed to Sadie. She had felt him there.

What used to be my body is in a place of honor, he relayed, letting me know that his cremated remains had been put in a place of prestige in the house. Sadie confirmed that the urn was on a mantle surrounded by happy photos.

Please reassure my human mom that what she planned to do with the ashes is a fine idea.

"For the last week we've been discussing what to do with the urn full of China's ashes," said Sadie.

Sadie was also turning her attention to living pets in her household.

The new puppy, JoJo, had a few problems, and one of them was barking. Sadie had tried some behavior modification techniques but nothing seemed to help.

China was still tuned in from his vantage point, so I asked him if he was willing to help with the new member of the family. He said he was happy to help by showing me pictures of "having a chat" with the new Yorkie to instruct him in the proper household behavior. The feeling was one of having a big brother around to show you the ropes. China volunteered to continue training JoJo about when barking was appropriate through "spirit visits."

A month later, Sadie let me know that the new pup's behavior had indeed improved: He only barked now when someone was at the door. She was grateful for China's help from beyond the physical plane.

The lesson that pets who have passed on are more than willing to assist with new members of the household was not lost on me. After my experiences with Sadie and China, I have often asked pets on the other side to help. They're always willing. Frequently, an aging animal will help communicate the "house rules" to a new pet before the older pet passes on. Even once pets have crossed over and are out of their physical bodies, their generous and loving spirits continue to help in any way they can. ☀

11

Sourdough Gets Lost

Helping find lost pets is one of the most difficult services I provide. A medium can bring images through of places an animal has visited or is looking at in the moment, but those pictures are often very common sights in a particular geographic area. Yet the rewards are tremendous when people and their beloved companions are reunited.

My first lost animal case was Sourdough the cat. I had resisted such cases because of the ambiguity of the messages. But I also knew that my Higher Sources would send me a case to practice on as soon as I was ready, and they did.

Sourdough's caretaker, Kathleen, was desperate. Sourdough had led a pampered life for 14 years and his lack of independent living skills worried Kathleen terribly. He often stayed out for a day or two, but Kathleen had recently moved and Sourdough had taken off. Now he was nowhere to be found.

I explained to Kathleen that pictures sent to me in these situations were often ankle-level (the pet's perspective) and didn't yield a lot of useful information.

When I tuned in to the fluffy off-white cat, I felt he had not wanted to make the trip to the new place, as he was quite content in his old neighborhood. As I closed my eyes and concentrated, sensing that he was not that far from home in his small Idaho town, I saw him near a red outbuilding and felt some female attention around. A nice woman was feeding him and scratching his belly.

Sourdough was on a kind of rugged camping trip, something very different from what he was used to, and had not decided whether to come home. In my vision, he walked along a country road dotted with power lines, enjoying his new adventure. Behind him there appeared to be a stand of what looked like eucalyptus trees.

When Kathleen said there weren't any eucalyptus nearby, I second-guessed that it was some kind of tree with shedding bark, since that element of the picture stood out.

"I'm going out today to look for places that fit your description," she told me.

Cared for by another loving female, the so-called Dough Boy may have decided to continue with his new life. I waited to see.

"Sometimes," I told Kathleen, "an animal decides to step aside to make room for another animal who needs a home. Call it a karmic debt or whatever, but I've seen it happen."

"I was thinking of getting another cat," Kathleen said. "I still have one left but she's lonely now."

"Wait for a few days to see what unfolds," I suggested.

By the end of the week, Kathleen and Sourdough were reunited.

In my visualization and communication with him, I created telepathic "crumbs" for the kitty to follow home if he wanted to go back. Uniting my vision with Kathleen's fervent wish for his return sent out a strong telepathic trail for him to follow: *If you want to go home, follow the trail of your mom's desire,* I relayed to him.

And when the romance of the open road faded for him, he headed home, empowered by his exploits.

* * *

Lost pets are common. Many animals are fearless, some are naive, and others are willing to trade their safety and security for great adventure, roaming randomly about. With people shattered by the loss and pets unable to read street signs, the images I receive are ambiguous.

Complicating matters further, animals will not return to a home where there is at least one resident who doesn't want them there, or (in the case of some cats I've met) where they are confined to an indoor environment for life: Imagine never experiencing the outdoors, your life centered around one indoor space. Now imagine sharing that space with other animals you may not get along with and you'll recognize why some animals strike out on their own. ☼

12

A Rotty Under Threat

Diane loved a sweet young Rottweiler, Siggy, owned by her son.

Her worry over the dog's well-being was almost palpable over the phone when she called from Idaho, making the connection to me through my column in an alternative health care magazine. Siggy's increasing level of aggression greatly concerned her, and although the dog had never hurt anyone, the family worried that his behavior would accelerate and become more dangerous.

"My son is moving to a place where he can't have dogs," she said, "and Siggy's growling and snapping means he has very little chance of being adopted by another family."

After checking in with Siggy, I explained to Diane that I had felt overcome with anxiety in my body—ready to explode.

"You know how it feels when you've been sedentary for a long time, and all you really need to do is get out and take a brisk walk?" I asked her.

I told her that that was the message I had received from Siggy. I felt the three-year-old needed emergency exercise.

A flood of stress, frustration, and anxiety washed over me as I continued to focus on the poor Rottweiler.

"He's been chained up since he was just a puppy," Diane confirmed.

Spending the most energetic time in his life chained up was obviously why his aggression was beginning to show.

"If your son and his wife can't provide a needed release for the dog, his behavior will get even more territorial and aggressive," I warned.

Recalling how Siggy had once gotten loose, Diane told me he had been lost for a couple of weeks and had never been the same since coming home. She wanted me to find out what had happened to him during his absence.

It was frightening to be out on the street, but also exhilarating,

71

he relayed, sending me pictures of people yelling at him as he dodged thrown objects, coupled with the sensations of running, exercising, and glorious freedom. But many people were afraid of his size and intimidated by his breed.

I trusted a boy who I approached, but then he hit me on the head with a stick, Siggy said.

A persistent throbbing on the top of my head translated this message. As I looked into Siggy's skull I saw a mild concussion and felt disoriented. That was his physical experience. There was also emotional trauma.

With his energy suppressed and his movement restricted once again, Siggy was now worse off than before because he'd tasted freedom. With no real experience other than being chained, he hadn't felt comfortable being totally free since he had no skills when it came to finding food. However, he now knew there *was* a big wide world out there filled with other dogs, good people, bad people, fun places, scary places—all making his confinement to a tree even harder for him to handle.

Furthermore, Siggy realized his home was not secure, and that his family was considering abandoning him. He'd done something wrong, he was sure of that, although he didn't know what, and the threat of homelessness hung around his neck like a weight. Although routinely fed and watered, he was a mess psychologically.

As our short session ended, Diane promised to get personally involved in exercising the dog and in finding him a new home where he could run, play, and exercise.

Just two weeks later Siggy found the perfect home when a young jogging couple adopted him. Because of their willingness to work with his problem behaviors while attending to his overwhelming need for exercise, Siggy blossomed into a wonderful canine companion who was finally part of a loving family.

*   *   *

Siggy is a good reminder that pets need more than just food and water: Prior to making a commitment that will last many years, people who adopt an animal must take that animal's full range of needs into account beyond food, water, and medical attention: human and animal contact, exercise, and the reassurance of a secure home.

Because dogs are pack animals, they suffer depression and psychological trauma when left alone, especially chained up in the prime of life. Put yourself in their place and imagine being a young, energetic creature with four or five feet of living space in which to express all of your energy. It takes a toll, and pent-up energy can easily be transformed into problem behavior.

Instinctively, canines feel most happy when they have at least a quarter acre in which to roam, but this need can be satisfied with daily walks where they explore other animals' territory.

And be assured that any animal whose home is threatened will show signs of trauma. I've yet to meet an animal who doesn't know when someone is considering getting rid of them. Because animals don't use words to express themselves, what we consider bad behavior is how they release some of the tension.

Our animal companions fully understand statements like "I'm going to send you to the pound" or "I'm going to have you put to sleep." Even if these are only thoughts not spoken aloud, the pictures played in your head will be understood by your pets.

With these messages you threaten them with homelessness, separation, abandonment, extended life in a small cage, or an unpredictable future that could include death.

How would you feel not knowing what was going to happen to you, powerless to change your fate? If you were a non-verbal creature, you might resort to communicating your stress through inappropriate behavior. ☀

73

13

Special Dogs, Special Needs

Siggy's confinement was intensified by isolation, but a houseful of rescue dogs in New Mexico with plenty of pack interaction also needed the remedy of regular exercise.

The four Albuquerque dogs were mostly terriers with some poodle mixed in, and they could be fighting terrors. Each had been abandoned, experiencing life in a variety of homes that didn't last long, fighting for position, lacking in proper training, and full to their little eyelashes with energy.

Their loving caretaker, Eileen, was a busy woman who arrived home at night tired from a day's work and seeking sanctuary. But her expectations were unrealistic. Each night she opened her front door to find a frenetic gang of dogs who had been eagerly awaiting their humans' return all day. The dogs had spent *their* day suppressing young energy, the tension building. In the end, they turned it on each other.

Eileen wanted me to talk the dogs out of expressing this pressure aggressively. But without regular exercise, these dogs would never be able to settle down and live harmoniously, either with each other or with their human companion.

Again and again my question was the same: "How are you doing at implementing a regular exercise routine?"

Eileen felt somewhat defeated. A 60-year-old woman with a bad hip and a stressful high-level job, she felt guilty and overwhelmed by the dogs' need for exercise. I finally asked her if she would consider hiring a neighborhood dog walker, something she hadn't thought of.

Since there were no dog walkers in her immediate area, we requested help from our Higher Sources, and it wasn't long before Eileen found a professional dog walker for the four dogs that also added a bit of training to their walking routines.

With regular exercise, the dogs were drained of excess

energy by the time Eileen arrived home at the end of the day, and they all enjoyed each other's company much more harmoniously.

*   *   *

Two other tiny terriers with a need for exercise became my clients in the winter of 2005, and each came with her own high-energy issues.

Yorkshire terriers average between six and nine inches in height and generally weigh between three and seven pounds. Zanna was closer to the three-pound mark, while Ellie weighed in at six pounds. The dogs' silky coats were fine and glossy, a dark steel blue from the back of their heads to the roots of their tails. They both had faces, chests, and feet of bright tan.

Yorkies are intelligent, confident, affectionate, lively, brave, and spirited, and both of these little ones claimed these characteristics. But the breed also comes with a warning from experts that these dogs shouldn't be spoiled. Learning to obey is not really one of the breed's strong suits, and Zanna and Ellie each definitely had a mind of her own.

The smart little dogs belonged to two ladies who were friends, having found a bond in their healing vocations. So Zanna and Ellie were also girlfriends—sort of.

Barely beneath the surface, and often above it, there was a jealous hostility on the part of Zanna. Whenever Ellie was seated on the lap of her human, Sherilyn, Zanna gave a warning growl.

Problems increased when Zanna's human caretaker, Felicia, went out of town for a week. Sherilyn babysat Zanna, and the little terrier "claimed" Sherilyn as her own.

Sherilyn was direct in her communications with the little dogs, separating them and giving them time-outs when they exhibited aggression. Their behavior was perfect while they were in her care.

But when Felicia returned from her trip, all of Sherilyn's work was undone. Felicia's communications were indirect and her rules were soft, so Zanna went back to her old aggressive ways of behaving toward other dogs.

Animals, like children, can be angels with strangers and little devils with their regular human companions, especially if their own people lack follow-through or training skills. And, for most dogs, in the face of a lack of physical activity, aggression intensifies.

*   *   *

Finally, some dogs have special needs that go above and beyond the fundamental requirements of companionship, discipline, and physical activity.

Jake was a pit bull mix abandoned at the entryway of a rescue organization called PAWS. Volunteers found him tied there to a light pole when they arrived for work in the morning.

After he was given food, water, and affection, he quickly made new friends with the PAWS employees, who soon realized that Jake was deaf. They managed to locate his family a few days later and were told he was unwanted.

But Jake's bad luck was about to change.

With the dedicated help of PAWS, a rescue was found that would be a second chance for the young dog. Jake began a journey that took an entire team of people days of planning to get him to Winthrop Harbor, Illinois, where a near-perfect foster home waited. There, he was taught sign language by a woman who dedicated her spare time to deaf dogs.

A member of a group called DDEAF (Deaf Dogs Education Action Fund), social worker Annette was also deaf.

"As a deaf child, I was often shut out by other children," Annette told me, "so animals became my best friends. I've always vowed to repay them for their kindness and I'm still repaying them. I don't expect this debt will ever be paid off but I'm fine with that."

From Annette, Jake soon learned the sign language for *sit, outside, no, potty, down, stay, drop it, leave it,* and *off.* All of these were to help prepare him for permanent placement.

But when Jake attacked another dog in her household, Annette quickly contacted me.

"Jake left a small gash on Hootch's ear," Annette said to me through a relay operator on the phone. "There was blood everywhere. Jake's in a crate right now, but he's not happy about it. It's a bad situation and we're trying to keep the dogs separate but Jake will have to come out of there to do his business."

The pictures I received of the household included several

dogs, and Jake let me know the fight was about territory, toys, and asserting dominance. His instinct was to fight for his place in the household, and part of this meant protectively guarding Annette. I also sensed a chemical imbalance with Jake that indicated a need for a rigorous exercise program.

Like Siggy, Jake felt very unsure of himself and his future, and fearful of abandonment. But these feelings were complicated and intensified by his deafness, which always made him feel off balance.

Still 90 percent of Jake's problem was a result of the lack of regular exercise. ❀

14

Bosley Protests

Threatened homelessness was part of the problem when it came to the case of 14-year-old Bosley, a lovely and charming Siamese cat owned by a couple who traveled extensively.

"We are having some behavioral problems with Bosley," Phil told me. "She's peeing by the door every couple of days. I'm not sure what started this behavior but I could wring her little neck.

"In the past, she occasionally peed in the entryway of the house, which seemed like retaliation for leaving her when we traveled. We've been taking care of our son's dog for a week, and this behavior is now happening two to three times a day.

"I've tried washing the area with a bleach solution, spraying with NO™ spray, and blocking the door with a big rug. Now she just pees right on the rug and onto the doorjamb. I'm at the end of my rope, and I'm seriously thinking about a final visit to the vet."

There were several things contributing to this kitty's bad behavior, not the least of which was the threat of death. Even when a new dog in the house is friendly, it can be stressful for a cat, especially one that's not sure of her place in the family. Stress can then weaken the body's natural immune system, opening the door for problems like urinary tract infections.

"How about a visit to the vet for a health check-up instead of euthanasia?" I suggested.

I also talked to Phil about the difference between cat noses and our noses. Air fresheners are for people, and odor reducers only change how the nose smells; they don't remove the odor.

The significance of Bosley urinating on the door was not lost on any of us. She wanted to escape outdoors when she felt threatened by the presence of the visiting dog, and felt abandoned when the couple traveled, always worrying about whether her people were leaving forever. They never offered her any reassurances, which I suggested they do, along with telling her when they would be back and who would be taking care of her while they were gone.

As it turned out, the problem was in fact partly physical. Phil discovered this when he finally took her to the vet a week later.

"She has a bladder infection,"" he told me. "The vet gave her an antibiotic to be administered twice a day. He thought that her peeing was probably part behavioral and partly due to the infection."

This was just what I had said, but it took a second opinion for Phil to finally act. If you've ever had a bladder or urinary tract infection, you know how that cat suffered every minute as she waited for medication. And her suffering was not only physical but also psychological because she was receiving images of neck wringing.

Phil planned next to clean the door area with a pine-smelling cleaner, which I cautioned him against due to its toxicity to pets. (Nausea is just one possible consequence of toxic cleaners.) Phil also planned to put Bosley in the garage during the day and in the house only at night until the medicine kicked in. I suggested the opposite for this wonderful kitty, who really needed a lot more personal attention, not less.

"Spend some extra time with Bosley when you're home," I implored, "and don't forget to tell her what you're doing and why. Please have a chat with her today to explain that (a) you know she doesn't like it when you're gone and you're sorry it makes her upset; (b) for you to be happy, you take these trips, but you love her and want her to be happy, too; (c) when you're gone you'll make sure she's well cared for; and (d) she needs to use only her litter box for her bathroom needs.

"You can also make a deal with her, Phil," I went on. "Consider using the garage as a time-out consequence instead of a threat, once the medication is fully administered and if she has another accident. Calmly tell her that when she goes outside her box, you'll now begin putting her in the garage for an hour each time. If she wants to be with you in the house, she needs to use appropriate house and litter box behavior.

"And remember that all communication needs to be in the affirmative. Let her know what you *want* her to do, instead of telling her 'Don't do this' or 'Don't do that,' or you'll be sending her confusing images of the undesirable behavior.

"Finally," I concluded, "before you talk to her, get yourself into a state of loving kindness instead of the state of frustration with her that you've been expressing. Pets pick up on our emotions more than we can ever possibly understand. Consistency and patience are the keys here."

To make a long story short, I convinced Phil to try a more natural cleaning product and to give his needy cat some quality attention. It had been years since he'd actually played with her, so his overriding thoughts about her were whether to put her down or let her live. Phil also promised to try communicating directly with her, as well as implementing some of the other behavior-changing tactics I recommended.

It was very satisfying that a few simple strategies resolved the behavior problems with this sensitive Siamese and saved her life. At my suggestion, they also resumed playing kitty games with her, making her feel loved and cherished. Phil and his wife decided not only to spare her life, but also to keep her in the family.

*   *   *

Domestic animals of every species react to human emotion in the home, almost as mirrors to the situation. If your pet is acting out, take a look at what is going on in the immediate environment that could be triggering tension.

I've often seen problems with newly acquired pets who are trying to establish themselves in a household of multiple pets; with animals like Bosley who are left alone for long periods of time; after a move to a new home; and, most sadly, adopted animals who are "on trial" or under the cloud of possible euthanasia.

All of these problems can create the kind of emotional stress that leads to physical or behavioral issues and, in turn, litter box difficulties. ☀

15

Snowberry's Sad Story

Bosley's story is very common when it comes to cats trying to get a message across to their human caretakers. As in Bosley's case, Snowberry also communicated by urinating in unacceptable places, and her humans, Rick and Cindy, were also travelers. A beautiful exotic Manx, Snowberry loved her human parents and wanted to please them, but felt lonely and abandoned when they traveled. To top it off, they forced her to take a nasty-tasting sedative that made her groggy and unstable.

Rick and Cindy left Snowberry alone for weeks at a time. She had a caretaker who stopped by every other day to spend a few hours with her, but she was lonely and anxious, and her humans were frustrated by her peeing in inappropriate places. After a visit to their local vet, Rick and Cindy decided to put Snowberry on kitty Prozac® to calm her fears. They had a Plan B if the sedative didn't work: euthanasia.

Snowberry hated the taste of the stuff, hopping around and drooling with each dose. But because the incidents of peeing on the front door stopped, her human parents claimed victory.

When I spoke with the cat, she showed me that she was being fed something she didn't like. In a session with her humans, I explored a couple of problems with the administration of the drug. Rick told me he gave it to her through a dropper. It had not occurred to him just to put it in her food—an easy solution.

The case frustrated me because other remedies existed besides drugging the animal. But unwilling to implement solutions that took more time and patience, Rick and Cindy found Prozac® a magic pill. Since the Manx lived with the threat of being killed, I naturally went along with the kitty Prozac® idea. Although the couple loved Snowberry, they wanted a labor-free cat and resisted trying less drastic solutions.

Earlier, we had tried another remedy to redirect the cat to the litter box: Rick and Cindy switched to the clumping kind of litter, which Snowberry liked much better, and she stopped having accidents. Then, all of a sudden, Rick and Cindy decided they didn't like the smell of the clumping litter in the garbage can, even though they sealed it in a plastic bag. They went back to the sharp-edged litter, and wetting outside of the box about once a month was the consequence. So they resorted to using the strong sedative instead of the new kitty litter.

At some point, and for unknown reasons, Rick and Cindy decided the kitty Prozac® was also too difficult to deal with and took Snowberry off it. Clearly, they were people who considered animals disposable, so I asked them to let me search for a new home for her before they again considered euthanasia. They agreed.

"I guess I was too optimistic about Snowberry," Rick said. "When she saw us packing to leave this morning, she peed on the door again. Anyway, I put her back on the Prozac®—gave her a dose this morning.

"I would appreciate it if you could help us find a home for her," he added. "I know no one wants a problem cat, but she might not be a problem somewhere else with people who don't do as much traveling as we do. I hate to put her down but I don't think I can live with this much longer."

Snowberry's people took drastic steps to have a customized animal that met their every need. De-clawing was one of those drastic steps. Instead of training the cat to confine scratching to appropriate places in the house like scratch poles, they had her front claws surgically removed.

This procedure involves amputating the last joint of each of a cat's "toes" (in human terms this is comparable to cutting off your fingers up to the first knuckle). Cats are crippled both physically and emotionally from de-clawing.

I've lost my sense of balance, Snowberry told me, *and I'm insecure without my natural defense mechanisms. Why did they mutilate my paws?*

I explained the best I could, but this sweet cat's survival was utmost on her mind and the damage to her paws was secondary. My heart ached for her because she told me she knew her life was threatened.

I put out an emergency e-mail to everyone I knew.

"One of my cat families travels a lot and their cat is

showing behavioral signs of being lonely," I wrote. "They plan to continue traveling and want what's best for their cat. But ultimately, the family has decided that both they and their kitty would be happier if she were in a home where she had more time with people.

"If you know of anyone who could give this wonderful and loving animal a home, please contact me. She's de-clawed on the front paws, playful, loves to be combed, has silky short hair, and is a healthy, petite 13-year-old female. She has been buddies with an extended family member's golden retriever, and is on one medication that is mixed into her canned food daily."

There was no response to my plea, but finally, Rick and Cindy got more consistent with their kitty Prozac® doses and the front-door peeing stopped, which made them decide to keep her.

I kept talking to her about how special she was, and how I and her kitty sitter cared about her and heard her pleas. I told her that Rick and Cindy also loved her but were ignorant of how best to take care of her. Soon afterward her kitty babysitter told me, "She seems happier now, more relaxed, and less upset about their being gone."

Loneliness is a lot easier to handle drugged. ☀

Kitty Prozac® Cautions

Kitty Prozac® is a prescription antidepressant that should be used only as a last resort. (Buspar®, an anti-anxiety medication, is also sometimes prescribed.)

Kitty Prozac® is used to treat obsessive-compulsive behavior such as constant licking in dogs and cats and feather-picking in birds, as well as aggression (although it can *cause* aggression in some previously passive animals). It may take one to four weeks before you see an effect. Worrisome side effects can include stomach upset, fatigue, anxiety, restlessness, panting, irritability, jaundice (yellowing of the gums, skin, or whites of the eyes), vomiting, or a persistent lack of appetite.

Your veterinarian is the only one who can prescribe this powerful drug and monitor dosage and side effects. Once you begin a drug regimen, don't suddenly stop it without consulting your vet first.

Before using it with a cat who is having litter box problems, consider the following:

- Rule out health issues. I've known people who punished their pets for urinating outside the box only to find that their animals had an infection.

- If all is clear on the health front, then the problem is behavioral, so first take steps to re-train the cat to the box. Try isolation in a small room with the box, some bedding, and food. When the cat starts to use the box consistently, increase the area it's allowed to ramble around in.

- Thoroughly deodorize wherever the cat has been eliminating. Nature's Miracle® is recommended.

- Try using Feliway® (available from your vet or pet store), a spray that mimics the happy scent cats leave when they rub their cheeks against something. Spritzing a little on the rugs keeps the cat from using them as a litter box.

16

Reggie Takes Charge

When Nancy called me about conducting a session with her German shepherd, Reggie, I asked her to send me his picture over the Internet. I planned to proceed with a typical telephone reading: the caretaker on the line, the pet's picture in my hand, myself, and all of our Guides, chatting together.

But the impact of Reggie's image moved me so deeply, and the soulful eyes that stared back at me from my computer screen drew me in so instantly, I knew I had to meet this wonderful dog in person. When I discovered during our initial chat that the family lived in my own community, I happily set up an appointment for an in-home consultation.

Nancy filled me in on Reggie's early life when I got there. He had spent his young energetic days with an active, noisy family with three children. He knew his job was to watch out for them, and he did it well. He was an outdoor dog, and his family traveled often, leaving Reggie alone, and much of the time tied to a tree. When off leash, he was confined by underground fencing that gave him a shock to the neck through his collar whenever he passed over it.

But Reggie's need for human companionship proved much stronger than the shock of the electric fencing. It didn't stop the young shepherd from visiting Nancy and her husband, who lived next door.

"He had many friends in the neighborhood, and at about the age of three or four, he would run right through the fencing to get to us," reported Nancy. "It broke my heart, and I would take the collar off so he could go back home without getting a shock.

"Before we moved next door, Reggie spent a whole summer tied to the tree," she said, "but he always had food and water and loved his family."

As the kids in Reggie's original family grew, their interests

85

turned to more active sports like swimming, running, and skiing. Eventually, their aging pet could neither go along nor keep up, so the family began to look for a younger, more energetic companion for their now-teenage children.

One day the neighbors told Nancy they wanted to come over to speak to her. It was an unusual request so she wondered what was up. Then the bomb dropped.

"I've accepted a job out of the area and we're going to move," said her neighbor. "We're not planning to take Reggie."

The family had found a young German shepherd who could go jogging with them, and they were planning to euthanize Reggie unless they could find someone who wanted him. Since he had so many friends in the neighborhood, they thought he might be happiest staying local, so they gave Nancy the first shot at adopting him. Horrified at the alternative, Nancy reluctantly took him in, then promptly fell head over heels in love.

After having the dog for about 18 months, Nancy had a few issues she hoped I could help with.

"We want to make sure that when we go away on vacation next week, he knows that we're not leaving him at the Pet Ranch for good, and that we'll come back and get him. We would never abandon him," she told me.

I talked to Reggie telepathically, taking him on a tour of the Pet Ranch in order to familiarize him with the facility. His loving human was sending him to the best possible place she could board him, I relayed. He would be well cared for, and he would be picked up as soon as Nancy and her husband returned. I also sent him the picture of spending a few weeks as part of a unique and changing pack. Finally, I reinforced the message to Reggie that he would not be abandoned and that he was greatly loved.

As I took the gentle dog around the Ranch in my mind, there was a sense of familiarity coming from him, so I told Nancy he knew the place. She confirmed that he had stayed there once before.

It was no wonder Nancy had called me in to reassure Reggie. His fear of abandonment was so profound that his emotions nearly bowled me over. Nancy said each day when she went to work her heart was heavy when Reggie would try to get into the car. He stuck like glue to her side as she got ready for work, his ears drooped, and he gazed at her with an expression of deep sorrow. She hated to leave him, even to go to the store. Even though she had been his caretaker now for more than a year, he still could not trust that she would return.

"Reggie needs a job," I told her. "I'll tell him that he's supposed to guard the house while you're away during the day, and that he's on duty. What I want you to do is to walk him around the perimeter of the property and show him the area he's supposed to guard. You can include the neighbor's house if you like, where his dog friend lives. Let him know you'll be back and that you're handing the house and property over to him while you're gone."

As I was leaving, Reggie's dog friend from across the street stopped over to visit, prompting Nancy to remember another issue she was dealing with. The dog was an 80-pound mixed-breed puppy—a combination of Great Pyrenees, chow chow, and Labrador retriever.

As he happily bounded toward us, Nancy said, "The problem is that the heavy puppy jumps up on Reggie, and I'm concerned about it causing him pain since he has arthritis. I want them to be friends, but I don't like the pup knocking him to the ground."

I asked Reggie about it and he showed me his perspective.

I can fix this problem, but it will get noisy, and I'm worried that it will disturb the humans, he told me. *I can teach the puppy some manners when it comes to respecting my space, but it will mean taking the youngster down to the ground a few times, and there'll be loud barking, growling, and a ruckus.*

"He would like you not to worry while he teaches the pup," I told Nancy.

Nancy gave Reggie the go-ahead to proceed with his plan, and over the next few weeks, it unfolded just as he had shown me.

"It was loud, and there was a lot of ruckus, just as you said," Nancy said, "but the pup's family was okay with it and he doesn't jump on Reggie anymore. The two dogs are much closer friends now."

Nancy also had another question for me to ask Reggie.

"Does he want to continue to exercise with me?" she asked.

"He says he can go part of the way, but not the whole way," I said, as Reggie showed me going on a walk and then resting in the car while Nancy continued with her exercise.

"He is saying he can go 'one,'" I translated. "I don't know

if this is one block, or one mile, but you will know. He says the exercise helps his arthritis."

Two months later Nancy reported that they were going around the block, and if she wanted to keep walking Reggie just slept in the car or back at the house while she continued. It was working out.

"Reggie is doing well," Nancy said happily. "I can't believe the change in him when I leave in the morning for work. Instead of a struggle with his wanting to go with me, he now sits on the front lawn, ears on alert, and just gives me a casual goodbye, as if to say, 'Go ahead and go. I'm on duty now.'

"He looks over his shoulder as I back out of the driveway, and sometimes he's actually at his dog friend's house across the street, the house I told him was also a place for him to watch. It used to be absolutely heartbreaking for me to leave in the morning, but I didn't think anything could be done about it."

During our session, I had also thought it wise to give Reggie a job at the Pet Ranch to keep his mind occupied while his folks were on vacation, so I let Reggie know that while there he would be in charge of watching over the smaller dogs and the family that ran the place. The results, according to Nancy, were entertaining and impressive. Reggie came home tired from his stay at the ranch.

"I think he tried to take care of everything and everyone during his stay," Nancy said with a laugh.

The owner, Kelli, reported that six German shepherds were staying at the Ranch that week. Reggie was the oldest of the group and acted the patriarch. A young female shepherd, Sheba, had been playing a ball-retrieving game with her caretakers, really enjoying the exercise. But when it came time to go inside, she wanted to stay outside and play, refusing to come in. Kelli called her and called her, but got no response. Eventually, Reggie went out, calmed her down, and herded her back inside, much to Kelli's amazement.

As our follow-up conversation came to an end, Nancy wanted to know one more thing—whether Reggie missed his former family and the action of youngsters in the household.

Her concern arose from a trip she had taken him on to visit his first family. She said he seemed so happy to see the children again, whining his excitement over and over. Nancy was afraid he missed them terribly, but I didn't share her concern.

"At this point, he appreciates the laid-back nature of living with you and your husband," I told her. "He remembers his other family fondly, but he is content with his life and very comfortable with all the love and amenities you've afforded him."

"He definitely seemed happy to go home with us when we got ready to leave," Nancy said, feeling reassured.

Reggie shot me a satisfied glance from his soft bed in front of the fireplace, then closed his soulful eyes and yawned as if to confirm that this was the good life. Never again did he worry about being tied to a tree or being considered disposable.

$$*\quad *\quad *$$

About three months later, Nancy prepared to travel again. Because the Pet Ranch was closed for a few weeks, she hired a dog sitter for Reggie, and she wanted me to have a chat with him about the situation. The sitter was due to visit that very evening, and Nancy asked me if I would participate telepathically.

Immediately, I began to talk to Reggie remotely. I showed him pictures of what he could expect: the woman coming over that evening, why she was there, what their relationship would be like over the upcoming few weeks, and pictures of his family traveling but returning home to him again.

Since I had been writing his story, I took time to tell him what an excellent job he had done at the Pet Ranch with his young dog friend and with his new family. I sent him lots of love and affection, relaying my admiration of his handsome countenance.

When Nancy called me a few days later, there was a smile in her knowing voice. She'd clearly seen the signs that I had been chatting with Reggie.

"The pet sitter also has several German shepherds," she told me, "but she was skeptical about what an animal communicator could do. I knew you'd been in touch already, though, because Reggie gets this intense look on his face. It's really in the depth of his eyes.

"He has been concentrating on something for the past few days, and he's been especially diligent at his job. When the sitter came over, he didn't bark at all. He was totally focused on her as she spoke, hardly taking his eyes off hers.

"'Do you think the pet psychic has already started talking to him?' the sitter asked me. I told her if you hadn't already begun, I'd be very surprised."

I confessed that I had begun our sessions a few days earlier, preparing Reggie for the change.

Nancy next took heartwarming steps in preparation for leaving Reggie at home while she went on vacation. She prepared his favorite homemade meals, plumped up his sizable bed with new cushioning, kept him up to date about her travel plans, and let him know she would communicate with him telepathically while she traveled.

*   *   *

Nancy is one of the most diligent animal caretakers I know, and she did everything in her power to minimize Reggie's fear of abandonment. Oftentimes, pets become fearful and nervous simply because they don't know what is happening.

During the same week that Nancy was getting Reggie ready for her time away, I consulted with another woman whose chihuahua, Tisha, was exhibiting strange behavior. The family was planning to move across country, making preparations to sell the house, showing perspective owners through the rooms, and beginning to pack.

As a result, the tiny dog was afraid she'd be left behind. Once she was better informed and reassured that she would be going along, she calmed down. Tisha's family found the transformation dramatic after one short session with me.

Reggie, on the other hand, was always well versed. Reinforcing Nancy's efforts by using my skill as an animal communicator further reassured him and clarified what would be taking place in the near future. He could not have asked for better vacation preps, and Nancy was rewarded with his faithfulness, protection, and love a hundredfold.

*   *   *

I recently contacted Nancy to see how Reggie was doing.

She told me he was aging gracefully, a little grayer, a little stiffer, but still able to make it up the stairs. Soon after my last session with them, Reggie took over patrol of his entire small neighborhood. Today he spends his days visiting the now-four-year-old Ben—the puppy he helped train not to jump on him—and watching his house from across the street at Ben's while Nancy and her husband are at work. ☀

17

Pythia's Egyptian Past

Every time I looked at the picture of Pythia the cat, I wanted to laugh out loud. I suspected she was telling me she was a very funny and entertaining kitty with a great sense of humor and mischief. The image showed her rolling on her back, and a picture came alive in my mind of someone touching her belly, causing her to sprint away.

I began my "chat" with Pythia by asking about her life before she came to live with her current caretakers, Sharon and Dennis. It took her some time to connect with a life before the current one, so I prompted her by asking if she were a rescue animal.

No, she said, showing me her picture as a very young cat, but a little older than a kitten, when she came to live in her present home.

Pictures of a woman feeding her played in my head, but I was also aware of autonomy—not in the sense of her being a feral animal, but in a lack of emotional attachment to her caretaker.

Did she love you? I asked her silently, a bit confused.

She took care of me, she said, *but not love like I get now.*

I would soon learn she had been fostered by a wonderful woman, so the emotional detachment made a lot of sense. Although she was being cared for, she knew she wouldn't stay there for good.

Tuning in to Pythia's body, I heard a message about problems with her eyes and an eye infection. She let me know that Sharon had helped her clear this up with medication. As my consciousness traveled down her body, Pythia seemed to have something on her back foot. She showed me a flicking motion cats make when they have an annoying piece of tape on one of their paws, like trying to sling it off, but she said it was no longer a problem.

Pythia also had a heartache, a childhood hurt centering around a lack of emotional bonding with her mom cat and people. She said she was learning to bond with people now and enjoyed the comfort of regular meals and a warm house.

I knead my humans and other cats because I didn't get enough time with my mom when I was just a kitten, she showed me.

As the session continued, a warm feeling came over me as I imagined myself down on the rug with her. I "felt" the luxury of Sharon's exotic rugs. Pythia loved the textiles, and I felt a blast of warm air as she luxuriated on the rugs, so I assumed it meant she parked herself in front of the heater or fireplace while rolling around on the carpets.

I understand that you enjoy the indoors. How do you feel about going outside? I asked her.

As I took her to the door in my mind's eye, she backed up, demonstrating she wasn't that keen about leaving the house, especially during bad weather. She liked the outdoors only when it was sunny. And she indicated that rain gave her the shivers as a chill washed over me accompanied by a picture of a downpour.

During our chat, Pythia really opened up, showing me that she loved to stalk. A bird and bug watcher, she also enjoyed hiding in a group of plants and annoying other cats by jumping out on them as they passed by. Sharing her more mischievous side, she said she had been caught scratching forbidden objects like the couch.

As I investigated how she interacted with her people, she said she preferred a little distance to sitting in a lap, and enjoyed perching on the back of the couch. When Sharon was sick and resting, she would join the other group of cats on Sharon's bed, but curl up farthest away from Sharon.

Pythia said she had a relationship with crystals and showed me a crystal in her water bowl. Fascinated by looking down into the water at it, she was able to tune in to the subtle energy of the stone, getting a physical boost from the radiating light.

As many cats do, she loved tree bark as a scratch post and enjoyed a good upward stretch. She told me she could be possessive of food and her food bowl.

I'm a daddy's girl, she said, showing me images of happily following Dennis around the house and outdoors.

As our chat came to an end, Pythia showed me earrings on her ears and a past life as an Egyptian temple cat. She liked jewelry and would definitely go for a fancy collar.

Notice my fancy white feet, she pointed out. *They're not like any other cat's markings here.*

After my session I asked Sharon to check Pythia's back teeth because I saw a potential problem there, but I didn't feel the difficulty required any immediate attention.

Here's what Sharon had to say about my reading:

"The earliest part of her upbringing is unknown. She came through the animal shelter at probably two weeks old. Weighing under two pounds, Pythia and her litter mates were to be euthanized, but two weeks later, at four weeks old, they were rescued by Purrfect Pals, a no-kill cat shelter.

"Then she went to a great foster home, and after that, two of them came to us.

"Yes, they were young, about four months old when we got them, and both were very, very affectionate kitties, possibly because they had been held like babies in the foster home.

"I don't know if Pythia had an eye infection earlier but it wasn't with us. However, you are 100 percent correct about the hind foot. She had a touch of ringworm on her hind toes when she arrived. Whenever I treated it with medicine, she would shake her foot as if there was a piece of tape on it. She had to stay in quarantine in the guest room for three weeks because of the ringworm.

"I would agree that she doesn't like to be out in bad weather, although her sister, Kali, doesn't mind. Pythia likes to ambush Kali in the very way you mentioned.

"All the cats like the back of the couch. Neither Kali nor Pythia are much for sitting on laps, but they do sleep by my head in bed and sometimes Pythia lies across my neck.

"I have lots of crystals in the house, and there's one in the cats' water bowl.

"She has never had tree bark for a scratching post, but I can certainly oblige her in that. She does like the upward stretch on the walls covered with fabric. She knows she's not supposed to scratch, but she does!

"Pythia lingers at the food bowl, unlike the other cats. This could be construed as possessiveness, but there is always food out so as to avoid competition. With five cats, they would never let me sleep in if they were expecting food. They all eat as much as they want whenever they want, and they don't overeat.

"Both Pythia and Kali have gum issues. The vet says they have juvenile feline periodontal disease, for which they have been treated. But it must always be watched.

"As far as the heart issue, Pythia is more aloof than Kali now, but they are both friendly. As babies they were both really affectionate, and Pythia still is, especially with my husband, Dennis, as you said. She does like to follow him around at times. But she is mostly a little snot to the other cats, except Kali.

"I certainly believe what you received about the jewelry, because she is a princess cat. I often speak to her on this subject because we already have Queen Tara in the house, so the princess must wait her turn at the throne."

Pythia and her sister, Kali—lucky cats who had found a loving pair of humans to care for their physical, emotional, and medical needs—were set for a lifetime.

Talking to and listening to Pythia illustrates the kind of reading in which a pet psychic simply opens up to hear what an animal has to share. It's difficult because most animals are not eager talkers, but for the most part they are very willing to answer specific questions. The animal communicator must still pose questions, but when there are no specific areas a human caretaker is inquiring about, the information that comes through is varied, addressing a wide variety of topics. ※

Section III

Public Bulletins

"Many have forgotten this truth, but you must not forget it. You remain responsible, forever, for what you have tamed."

~ Antoine de Saint-Exupéry (1900 – 1944)
French author (The Little Prince) *and aviator*

18

Television Newsmaker

Nearly a decade of conducting private readings for people and their pets, along with miraculous outcomes resulting from some of those sessions, gave me the confidence I needed to take the next step in my evolution as a full-time psychic counselor.

Summer brought a feeling of waiting for something new to happen. My fate firmly in the hands of my Higher Sources, I took a huge leap of faith, and went public—very public—and "coming out" was scary.

The marketing department at PetCo, a major pet store chain, was hosting two grand opening events at a couple of Washington stores, and they asked if I would do pet readings.

The first store appearance was a seven-hour drive away in Spokane, where I also contacted SpokAnimal, one of the animal rescue groups in the area, about teaming up for a fundraiser while I was in town. Their wonderfully competent public relations person, Lori Humphrey, went right to work, booking me on both a morning television show and a radio program, and arranging newspaper coverage, too.

For the television show, Lori planned for me to read the weatherman's dog, Doppler, so I spent some meditation time connecting with him to prepare for the appearance. Nervously, I realized my competence was going to be on the line—and on the air.

Arriving at the station at 5:45 a.m., I learned that the television and radio stations shared the newsroom. On the TV side, there had been changes as to which dog was to get a reading after several station employees argued on behalf of their own animal getting "psyched out." So despite my preparation, I discovered that Doppler would not be my sample pet. Ruger, the dog belonging to the television crime reporter, won the toss and arrived at the station about the same time I did.

The lights of computer screens, monitors, and network feeds filled the busy newsroom. However, a solitary silvery-blue fish in a tiny round bowl caught my eye as I waited to be called. Swimming in murky water, the beta fish sent a signal as clearly as if someone had tapped me on the shoulder.

I'm hungry and lonely, he said, as the movie in my head played a scene of the little fish swimming with a buddy and having some toys to swim through and around, like a castle. I made a comment about the fish having a message, and the anchors immediately put the flowery-finned fish in line for a reading. Little did I know the fish reading was going to be a lesson in caretaker sensitivity.

During an early break, the television news anchor came over to ask me if I could do a reading of her cat from a video. When I said I could, Cleopatra joined the list of waiting animals.

Because Ruger would be my first reading, my focus turned to him as we waited. Both of us were distracted by four other dogs in the busy newsroom, including mine and three others there to show off their Halloween costumes for the camera. There was lots of high anxiety on the part of the costumed dogs, whose vision was impaired by the clothing. They were also being exposed to a new and very busy environment, and each other, for the first time.

Nonetheless, the excited Ruger hurriedly told me he had been rescued by his caretakers, that his life had taken a turn for the better, that he was now well-loved, and that his present family was training him, a new activity he'd never experienced before. He also showed me a picture of being surrounded by newspapers in the yard. I made a mental note of his messages, and turned to the next animal in line.

The video of Cleopatra, the anchor's cat, showed her approach a tiny basket, step in, and curl up into a ball. This was surprising since the basket seemed way too small for her to fit in, but she snuggled in comfortably. In the next scene, the anchor's husband came into view, picked up the basket, and took Cleo on a ride, swinging the basket around in the air as his wife protested off camera.

The anchor's teasing husband was chanting "Wheee, wheee!" as Cleo flew through the air on a roller coaster ride, sideways and around.

Viewing the video, I visualized Cleo, along with a connection to both of our Soul-level Guides.

How do you like riding through the air in the basket? I asked her telepathically.

She sent me a profound feeling of trust.

My dad is careful and I know he won't let me get hurt. I'm safe and it's fun, she said.

What would you like me to tell your mom today? I asked.

I come between my mom and dad, she said, showing me pictures of sleeping between them and of being curled up in her female caretaker's lap. *I sometimes get in the way.* I thanked her for sharing the information.

When it was my turn to be interviewed, I stepped up onto the set, positioning myself next to the male anchor, who would do the interviewing. After telling the audience what I'd picked up about Ruger, the anchor then called Ruger's caretakers to the set to discuss the accuracy of the reading.

On camera, to my great relief, they announced that my reading was accurate regarding the dog's rescue and recent training.

They had found Ruger wandering around the neighborhood. They put him back in the yard where they thought he belonged, but it didn't take him long to escape and return to their house. When they tried to take him back again, they found old newspapers and undelivered mail. Neighbors reported that the family had moved, leaving Ruger to fend for himself, so the TV reporter and his wife decided to keep him. They had recently begun to train the sweet dog, an activity obviously new to him.

Cleopatra was next.

"What did you pick up about Cleo?" the female anchor asked me.

When I told her that the main message from the cat was that she "came between" her and her husband, the anchor gasped.

"The whole conflict of my life is trying to balance the attention I give to my cat with the attention my husband needs," she said. "I'm always trying to figure that one out, and she definitely comes between us. My husband jokes about it."

So far, so good.

Next came the beta fish, who belonged to the morning radio anchor. The producer called her over to the set. Her first comment offered immediate insight into why the fish felt hungry, lonely, and bored. He had been an unsolicited gift.

"This fish just won't die," she said laughing. "I've had it

for four years."

When I told her of the little animal's desires, she became immediately defensive.

"He'd like a toy to swim through, like a castle, and a fishy friend," I told her, "along with a little bit more clarity in the water."

"He *has* a rock, and I get him special water and warm it up every week," she said, annoyed at his demands. "Beta fish live in murky water in rice paddies, so I would think he would like the filmy water."

I felt it would compound her frustration to mention her fish's hunger, so I held my tongue, deciding instead to look for an ally in the newsroom willing to slip the fish a bit of food. I was later successful at getting the fish fed, but I had to leave the decision to care for his psychological needs—or not—to his caretaker. That encounter was a good lesson for me on compromise.

Publicity tour done, television news show goals accomplished, and my abilities validated on the air all fueled me for the next day's work as a pet store psychic. Long lines of people waited to talk to me. I was determined to keep my confidence intact even in the face of doubt—more of a challenge on some days than others. ☀

19

Pet Store Panacea

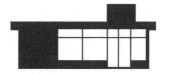

My work at the pet store consisted of four hours of 10-minute readings. More than once, my self-confidence was trampled as I relayed messages to people who shook their heads "No" as I spoke.

But I now found such reactions easier to take. When I first started doing readings, negative responses had thrown me off. I second-guessed myself, the messages I received, and whether I had chosen the right profession. *Maybe I'm not supposed to be doing this,* I questioned with trepidation in the direction of Heaven. But the clients just kept on coming.

In the midst of doubt, I received help from psychic John Edward by watching his television show, "Crossing Over," and by reading his books. Thank God/Goddess for this author, psychic, and internationally known television host. His courage at pursuing his craft in public, the skeptical comments I've heard from non-believers on and off the air, and the sacrifices he's made as a result of listening to his Guides and changing careers, give him a special place in my heart.

Watching John validated my own experiences with clients, making it more clear how the process of telepathic communication actually operates. He taught me that it can take weeks and even years for clients to validate information that comes through in a session. That fact alone proved very valuable as I moved tentatively forward, transforming a 20-year hobby into a full-time vocation.

PetCo had again hired me to provide free 10-minute readings for their grand opening celebration, and subsequently I worked for them all across Washington state in the same capacity. Although it was difficult to get a sense of an animal and its needs in such a short time, especially with all the distractions, the challenge was usually rewarded with happily astonished customers.

But sometimes, with rows and rows of treats, toys, and food immediately behind me, the animals found themselves in a stimulating and unfamiliar environment where they were curious, excited, and interacting with each other while standing in line. Some messages confused me—like the dog who told me emphatically that he was the only dog at home, when in truth he had a brother. I wondered if he were trying to tell me something was about to happen to his dog brother. Or was he saying he was the only dog that really mattered?

Because I had a table in front of me, people often placed smaller animals upon it to begin the session. As a result, I spent several minutes immediately reassuring some of the more nervous pets that there would be no needles or body probings involved in what was about to happen next.

The skeptics came out in force to these public readings. "Free" was an open invitation for the unconvinced to come and experience my work without any investment in the outcome. Some were like the stone-faced woman with a golden retriever who sat opposite me waiting to prove me wrong. I could feel the tension, and her crossed-arms attitude made it difficult for her dog to share what was on his mind. Because she was obviously very private and also doubtful of my abilities, her dog did not feel free to talk. With the first words out of my mouth, her head began to shake "No." It felt like judgment day in front of a stone execution wall.

A deceased white pit bull named Duff also presented a puzzle. He told me he was seven years old, but as I spoke those words his caretaker shook her head. She had presented a picture of the dog as the reading began, and finally told me he was two and a half in the picture. But the picture was four years old, and Duff's exact age was unknown. My confidence teetering, I explored further, only to find out that, had he lived, he currently would have been about seven.

The overall impression I got from Duff was that he was simple—simply happy, easy to love, easy to please, enjoying simple pleasures like lying in the sun or going for a walk, all of which his caretaker confirmed. I felt his childlike innocence most profoundly, and felt that it had been the cause of his demise. The woman revealed that Duff had experienced brain damage as a pup, after his mother had nearly smothered him and humans had breathed life back into his little body. Happily but inattentively moseying along, sweet Duff had ambled into the street and been fatally hit by a car.

Next in line was a striped male kitty waiting to chat with me. The woman with him handed me a picture that showed him in a kitty-sized easy chair. His message to me was *I'm king of this castle.* After the reading, the woman shared with me that the tabby was living in a house she and her husband had bought. When his original family moved away, he refused to go with them. Adopted by the new tenants, he was living a good life in the castle he had refused to vacate!

The cat's message further confirmed the simplicity of how animals communicate. Often, they don't go into great detail about what they mean or how they came to have certain views. They simply relay a one-phrase message, and it is up to me and their caretakers to figure out what they mean. It is in the interpretation of the words and pictures the animals send that psychics are most vulnerable to relaying the wrong message. "I'm king of the castle" could have been interpreted in several ways.

The following weekend I traveled to Mount Vernon and set myself up in PetCo's next grand opening location. Lack of promotion and advertising made the event an easy one, in the sense that very few people knew about the free readings. The employees, who had brought pictures of their beloved pets, turned out to be the main beneficiaries of my services there. But those who did stumble onto me were happy with my services. I felt blessed with the lighter workload.

It had been an intense few weeks and I had accomplished quite a bit: My first nerve-wracking television appearance was behind me. I was now an on-call psychic for a well-known chain of stores. And, most importantly, I had new armor for dealing with skeptics and expanded experience in bringing messages through from animals and quickly switching focus in 10-minute increments. ✸

20

Bichon Bash

Summer appearances at popular events continued, and the August heat played with mirage images on the asphalt of the road as I headed west to the Bichon Bash, a fund-raiser arranged to support *Small Paws Bichon Rescue* and fight abuse and neglect of these white powderpuff dogs. It would be quite the learning experience for me—one that would reassure me further as well as teach me that even under the most difficult circumstances my Higher Sources were willing to do their part in helping me convey information.

Arriving an hour and a half late due to a scheduling mix-up unnerved me since I'm a punctual person, but it didn't seem to deter the relaxed crowd sitting in lawn chairs scattered around a half-acre play yard filled with bichons. The homey set-up was a small speaker and a hand-held microphone sitting on front-door steps. The audience was about 25 feet away from me under several awnings.

Without a podium, I had to choose between holding my eight-page speech or the microphone. The mic won. I set my speech down on the steps and regrouped, ready to give an improvisational talk while glancing at the papers at my feet and trusting that I'd remember the outline.

The wind immediately blew my pages away. Scrambling after them mid-speech, then finding a rock to serve as a paperweight, I continued to talk. Meanwhile, my patient and tolerant Rusti was being hotly pursued by a dozen small bichons, all with their noses firmly pressed into her rear as she tried to get away and position herself near me. One of the dogs barked shrilly and relentlessly at Rusti as I spoke. Finally, its caretaker got up and removed the noisy animal.

I ended up cutting my talk short, since the whole situation proved impossible as a speaking engagement. It occurred to me that I needed to make a list of the things I would require from event organizers in the future. Light-bulb moment.

I did manage to incorporate Rusti's story into the talk. I also provided information about how telepathy works, how people can talk to their own pets, and examples of this type of communication in everyday life. I gave the audience a brief synopsis of my broadcast background for the wrap-up, and then the hostess invited those who had signed up for private readings to begin the procession into the house, one by one.

The hostess had told me that my readings would take place in the sunroom, which sounded like a garden paradise over the phone. The room was indeed a beautiful Casablanca-like setting, with white wicker furniture, lots of windows, glass double doors at the entry, and a light, airy feeling. Clients could either sit on a love seat opposite me or in a wicker chair next to mine.

When the first couple took their seats with their little bichon, I suddenly became more aware of my surroundings: People were going in and out of the kitchen in back of me, turning water faucets off and on. Other dogs entered the house and even the garden room, which had walls on three sides but a back that opened directly onto the kitchen and a hallway leading to the bathroom. Several people made trips down the hallway, and on the other side of the glass doors where clients entered a woman sat on the couch with the television turned on to a volume appropriate for the hard of hearing.

I soldiered on.

It had been only a week since I'd written a short note to my mentor, Patty, asking her if I would ever develop the confidence I needed to do psychic work effectively, but my first client of the afternoon would demonstrate that I was well on my way. She asked me about her dog's fear of riding in the RV. The dog didn't seem to have a problem with the regular car, but when I visualized him in the RV, he gave me the feeling that he didn't understand why the living room moved. He experienced nausea as a result of the moving vehicle, along with confusion about why things outside the window rushed by.

The moment I began to relay these feelings, the woman began to shake her head.

"That can't be it," she kept repeating. "He just started this behavior."

But this time, instead of second-guessing the information, I simply asked the animal's Guides and my own Teachers to show me the message again, and they did. It was the same one. I summarized the session by repeating what I had received and the nervous, high-strung woman left, still shaking her head no.

"Off to a great start," I muttered to the unseen, but Spirit was trying to show me how far I had come in my confidence quotient.

Another dozen people waited to see me, and I secretly hoped the rest of them were a little more open to the messages coming through. They were. My Spirit Guides would not test me beyond my limits, and I passed this one by not allowing my rocky beginning to color the experiences I had with the other waiting dogs.

I could not diplomatically share the whole truth about the first little bichon, though. The message I held back was that his caretaker was wound up as tight as a clock and his little body was extremely tense. I suspected that his home was not a place of great harmony. When I touched him he nervously rubbed his nose on my palm. Feeling his tail, a common place where dogs store tension, was like touching a live electrical wire. I suggested that his family dissipate some of the tension there by stroking his tail and imagining a blue healing light as they petted. But I doubted that they would follow my prescription.

Several people had problems with their pets in the car. Others wanted to know what kind of abuse their animal companions had suffered prior to their adoptions. Some wanted to know if their dogs wanted to be show dogs, and there were dog and food aggression issues as well.

The afternoon wrapped up with my host and hostess joining me for a reading with their little pet, Stormy. He was a sweet little bichon who adored his human parents, and a good little communicator, too, sending me pictures that were quite clear. I closed my eyes to get a better "look" as Gordon asked me why Stormy liked high places.

"I can see him walking on the back of the couch," I began, "and ending up behind your head. He feels very secure and protected by you there. He says he is also able to see the entire room and to keep an eye on things from there."

"Suzan," my hostess said softly, "look."

When I opened my eyes, Stormy was seated at the back of her chair right behind her head. I looked and laughed, then closed my eyes again.

Gordon then asked me why the pooch sat in his lap most of the time. "He's my wife's dog," he said, "and we want him to sit with her."

Gordon was a tall man and Stormy conveyed the feeling of really being able to stretch out on his lap. It was a very long lap, and as his tiny paws hung over the side of Gordon's leg, the bichon's body stretched out to its full length. When I opened my eyes again, Stormy had crossed the room, jumped into Gordon's lap, and demonstrated what a great lap he offered!

A few days after the reading, I received this e-mail message from my hostess:

"Suzan: You told Stormy to spend more time on my lap and HE IS DOING JUST THAT! Thank you so much. We can't believe it! He will leave Gordon even when Gordon is having a snack and come lie with me for a while and then go back to Gordon. It's a miracle! — Bonnie" ☀

21

Psychic Radio

My first chance to go back to where I had spent the majority of my first career in radio came six months after living in the Pacific Northwest with my new husband.

Homesickness was crippling me, so when an opportunity came up to go home to California's Central Coast for a few days, I jumped on it. I planned a full agenda concentrated on spending time with dear friends, including Dave Congalton, a radio talk show host with whom I had worked for several years.

Hired at the station where I worked as the news director and a talk show host for more than 10 years, Dave was a Ph.D. and former college professor. He was popular because he wasn't afraid to rattle cages or take people to task. He spoke with senators and congressional members, business advocates, events organizers, and arts aficionados. Although psychic phenomena were not one of his interests, he invited me on his program anyway.

As a former talk show host, I missed my audience powerfully, but this time I was on the other side of the microphone as a guest instead of an interviewer. And not only had I changed sides of the table, I was also "coming out" to a community who previously knew me only as a newscaster and talk show host.

I was also concerned about doing readings on the air. The nature of a psychic reading is predictive to a great extent, which leaves a lot of room for clients to wonder what you're talking about. It's impossible for people to validate what a psychic is saying when the event has yet to happen. With just a few minutes allotted per caller, it can also be tricky if the host of the program is looking for validation. Because Dave was skeptical about the psychic realm, I knew it would be challenging. I was putting one of my most prized possessions on the line: my credibility.

ABC News from New York played at the top of the three o'clock hour, and the computer began Dave's theme music at exactly 3:06 p.m.

Dave opened the microphone, introduced himself, teased the audience with the day's topics, and turned to me.

"Many of you may remember Suzan Vaughn from when she was the news director and a talk show host here at KVEC. About six months ago, she married the man of her dreams and moved to Washington state.

"Suzan has always had an interest in psychic phenomena, and that's why we always had the news first here at KVEC when she was the news director," he joked.

He explained that it wasn't something he believed in, then offered his audience a chance to get a free reading on the air.

I kept my eyes shut during the time I took calls so as to "see" and "feel" images better.

One of the first callers, a woman who had had a falling out with someone close to her, wanted to know if the conflict would be resolved soon.

I sensed she had a problem with her child, and she confirmed it involved her daughter. I told her I felt that she and her daughter had been very close, and that this conflict basically centered around her daughter's wish to break free of her mother's influence. It had a kind of "teenage" energy of rebellion around it, even though I felt the girl was older.

I advised her to take a few steps back and wait a few weeks before sending a "Thinking of You" card. Feeling the pain of separation between the two who had once been very close, I reassured her that they would be close again, once the daughter asserted her independence.

The woman confirmed the accuracy of my reading and thanked me.

Then a man called to ask about his stocks. I did not believe that psychic information, at least in my case, would be given to me to blatantly advance someone's material gains, but I had already made my agreement with my Higher Sources. My readings were "for the highest good of all concerned," and if this were in the best interests of this man, so be it.

"I'm not sure this kind of information will be available to me, but let me take a look and see," I told him.

I "saw" three bar graphs and he told me he had three stocks. One of the bar graphs was quite low, the next was about halfway up to the top, and the third was filled in completely. As I watched, all three vertical bar graphs filled with color that ascended to the top.

I sensed the man should keep his money where it was invested and I told him so. (In the next few days the stock market went up by over 200 points.)

Another interesting caller was a young man named Brian, who started with a question about psychic phenomena.

"I'm skeptical," he said. "I don't really think any of this is true. So I was wondering if you could say something that would make me less skeptical, or if you could change my mind."

"You're asking whether I can do anything to make you less skeptical," I said, "and the answer is no. The truth is, Brian, I don't feel it's my job to convince you, and I wouldn't try. I can tell you doing readings is very God-centered, and it requires meditation, trust, and practice. But it's just another form of communication, and anyone can develop his or her ability to communicate in this way."

He was a little taken aback, saying "Oh," so I went on.

"Do you have a question for me anyway?" I asked.

He came back to life.

"Yes, I do. I want to know where you see me in a job. Will I get one and what will I be doing?" he asked.

"I see you at a drawing table, the kind that swings back and forth," I told him. "I guess that's a drafting table, and you seem to be drawing.

"You are in a work setting, and I'm also hearing 'CAD'— computer-assisted design of some kind. I don't feel that this is a long-term job, but a first job, from which you will enter the workforce and begin a career."

"So what do you do, Brian?" Dave interjected from the host chair. "What are you studying?"

"Mechanical engineering," said Brian.

Dave threw his fists in the air and declared, "We have a psychic in the building!"

We laughed.

Phone lines were lit up for the whole hour, and so many people wanted to get in on the free reading that Dave extended the program.

The many callers renewed my spirit. As I drove away in

my rental car, the land was still green from recent rains. I smiled and breathed in the fragrance and the beauty of open pastures and rolling hills through Carpenter Canyon, satisfied that another public appearance has gone very well indeed. ☀

Section IV

Equine Communiqués

*"The wind of heaven is that which
blows between a horse's ears."*

~ Arabian Proverb

22

Teacup and Chestnut

The most surprising thing I have learned as an animal communicator is that the horse is one of the most psychologically abused of all animals.

Because they are expensive to keep and require a tremendous amount of professional care and attention, horses are often asked to do things that either produce a return on that investment, or perform according to the vision of the purchaser.

People with specific agendas write the hefty checks. Riding, hunting, rodeo, roping, driving cattle, jumping, cutting, and dressage are names for just a few of the planned activities humans have for their significant equine investments. Sometimes horses say no to those plans. And sometimes, they're willing to participate in these activities for years, but come to a point when they're done.

Teacup, a seven-year-old gray mare who was retired from racing, wanted nothing more than to become a mother. That's what she had always wanted. When I connected to her, the emotion in me rose from my heart to my eyes, and tears flowed. Composing myself in order to go on with the reading took a few minutes.

"I'm feeling loss, separation, and a great deal of sadness," I told Kurt, the man who had purchased her once she was retired. "I see other horses she considered part of her herd being sold, moved, and transferred. Stall locations were changed without thought for her need for closeness with other animals she loved, and young horses were taken away without explanation. I do see one live birth for her that made her extremely happy, but she says the humans involved were angry about it and the foal was immediately taken away, even before it was weaned. Injections dried her milk so she could

117

race again. That was a very difficult time for her. Her rebellious attitude started just after that."

Teacup's uterus was subsequently sewn shut so she wouldn't become pregnant again.

I'm a fighter because I've had it with insensitive people ordering me around, Teacup told me.

Kurt had enlisted my services to better understand why Teacup fought with him at his every request, and to let her know she could trust him. "When I approach her with an open heart she gets even more feisty," he said. "It's like she resists love. I want her to know it's safe here and I won't force her to do anything she doesn't want to."

The information that flowed between myself and Teacup included sending her the joyful feeling that results when horse and rider move in a flow of harmonious energy, encouraging subtle communication leading to graceful movement. She embraced the pictures I sent her, showing me she was willing to do her part in making that happen.

Like people who have been damaged by life, Teacup had also showed me that the pain of loss, abandonment, separation, and vulnerability made her nervous.

She told me she had recently been moved to a new boarding stable. She preferred the old one where there were green rolling hills and other horses she liked, but her caretaker had relationship problems with the owners of that facility.

One day I cooperatively got into a horse trailer and all of a sudden I found myself separated from my friends and in a whole new place. I can't take it anymore, she told me.

I explained that while her new place had more dirt and less grass, Kurt hoped it would be more peaceful for both of them since there had been a great deal of disharmony with the owners of the previous boarding stable.

Kurt also told me that in Teacup's new stable she was beginning to make friends with a thoroughbred gelding a few stalls down named Chestnut.

I like him but he can't be trusted, Teacup told me. *He's all keyed up and he would bite and kick if he were let out of his stall.*

Each night when Kurt visited Teacup, he led her to the door of Chestnut's stall so the two horses could touch noses.

"I'm sure Chestnut will belong to me someday," Kurt told me.

"I am too," I assured him, "but for now, that's not necessary for you to help him get what he needs. Continue

118

bonding with him, then we'll move to the next step of getting him out of that stall."

The pictures Teacup sent me matched my own vision that Chestnut could not yet be trusted when it came to aggression, and it was too early to allow the two horses to play together in the open fields. The gelding was experiencing one of the worst kinds of abuse for a high-energy, physically fit horse.

"What's happened to him?" Kurt asked me.

"His body feels like it's about to explode with pent-up energy," I explained. "Depression and frustration are causing him to eat the wood in his stall, and kicking the walls is a message that he's desperate to get out. I hope as both of us work with him he can calm down a bit so you can let him out to run. He needs that more than anything."

Chestnut had been a racehorse too. His former person, for unknown reasons, had abandoned him at the boarding facility. The facility owner was a kind-hearted elderly woman who made sure he had food and water, but she wasn't able to do much more.

Confinement to a stall for more than six months had taken its toll on Chestnut. Kurt wanted to get a halter on him, making it possible for the thoroughbred to get out and run.

If you will allow Kurt to put a halter on you, it will lead to freedom and a long run in the pasture, I told Chestnut. With that, I did some healing work on him to release some of his stagnant energy and calm him down.

It took a few months of working with Chestnut, but Kurt was finally able to get him into a bridle and out into the pasture.

Chestnut ran. He kicked. He was hard to get back into the stall. "Don't worry," I told Kurt. "Just allow him to be out for a while."

A few days later, after the beautiful thoroughbred got some desperately needed exercise, he returned to his stall to eat, after being reassured that he would be allowed back outside.

Soon it was safe to introduce other horses to him, including Teacup, fulfilling his deepest desire to become part of a herd once again. The gray mare showed me that the two of them would make a great parenting team, and Kurt promised to have her bred.

Teacup's communication about wanting to be a mother seemed defeatist at first.

I've lost hope of becoming a mother, she told me.

It's still possible, I told her. *It's okay to keep your dream alive.*

Her countenance brightened. She believed these promises in part because Kurt had had the stitches removed that prevented her from birthing a foal. He promised to consider breeding more seriously in a year or two when he could better afford another horse. Teacup's strong desire for a foal gave us what we needed to negotiate the behavioral changes Kurt was seeking and she was soon a much more cooperative horse.

As the session ended I told Kurt, "Because Teacup has allowed me to channel some of her grief, you'll be seeing a different animal when you visit her tonight." And he did.

"There is a big difference in my mare," he told me. "She is a lot softer, quieter and more cooperative. She trusts me much more now and doesn't fight me when I ask her to do something." ❁

23

Rountree Relaxes

Kaleb's horse Rountree was spooked by pavement. Whenever horse and rider approached a road, the horse sometimes backed up and refused to step on the road and other times ran at full gallop to get across the pavement as quickly as possible.

I told Kaleb to communicate telepathically with Rountree long before getting to the road.

"Send him telepathic pictures of what you expect before you get to the road," I instructed. "While you are riding toward the road, your head is filled with pictures of the behavior you don't want from him accompanied by your own anxiety. It's reinforcing the behavior you don't want and raising his level of anxiety."

"Please tell him to respond to my signals even when he's afraid," Kaleb said. "I want him to know I will protect him and I won't take him into harm's way. He needs to trust me and to develop some impulse control."

Rountree relayed a message back to Kaleb.

"He wants you to know it will take time to get past some of his fear," I said, "and some of it may never go away, so you will need to keep the dialogue open and flowing.

"You can tell him out loud, 'We will be approaching the road in a few minutes. I will give you a signal by stroking your neck, then a soft kick when it is safe to cross the road. I need you to walk across the road calmly. I am trusting you by not using a bit. I also need to feel safe with you because you are much larger than me.' When you speak to him out loud, your telepathic pictures will follow your words."

A few days later Kaleb reported improvements.

"Please tell Rountree I was thrilled at how well he did

today on our ride. It made me more confident to feel him so relaxed, swinging his whole body," Kaleb told me. "Before he came to me, he was worked way too hard, hauling elk shot by hunters and working cattle."

In a few weeks I heard from Kaleb again.

"There's something else your horse friend wants me to share with you," I told him, after tuning in to Rountree.

"Rountree is showing me his goofy side, which has been suppressed up to now and is about to re-emerge. This is related to flapping his lips. He asks that you watch for this behavior and play along," I translated.

"I have been giving him extra carrots, and about a week ago he did play with me with his upper lip," Kaleb told me. "I am surprised that our relationship turned around in less than a year. I was prepared to spend two years, or longer, waiting for him to come around. This is really great." ☀

24

Danny's New Life

Danny, a satin chestnut thoroughbred who lived in Montana, opened up to me right away as the information flowed freely. Sending him loving feelings for several hours before my phone session with his caretaker, Dallas, had been a big help.

You certainly are beautiful, Danny. Are you a show horse?

Yes, he said. *I am tired.*

Do you stand around and look pretty or do you actually perform?

I perform. With that, he showed me a picture of standing in front of a row of jumping bars, but not jumping over, which confused me.

Where do you live? I asked.

I live in a stable with other horses, apart from my human mom. A woman takes care of me there, he said.

Can you show me the source of your feeling tired? I asked.

Yes, he said, directing me to his neck area.

What is your favorite food? I asked.

He showed me that it was something small, red, and round.

How are your feet? I asked.

One of them is healing, he relayed, showing a picture of an antibiotic salve on the place where the hoof connects to the right front leg.

"Would you like me to tell you what information he sent me first?" I asked Dallas as my session with her began.

"Yes, let's start there," she said.

I started by telling Dallas that Danny felt tired and I suspected he had a thyroid problem.

"The vet says that one of his thyroid glands is swollen more than the other but it's not a big deal," she said.

"Danny says his favorite food is small, round and red," I went on, "so I'm taking that to mean either grapes or peppermints."

"Peppermints," Dallas confirmed. "He is boarded at another farm away from me and a woman takes care of him there."

I told Dallas about my confusion related to his ambiguous picture of standing at a bar for jumping but not going over.

"He has jumped but he's not doing it right now," she said. "He's had a foot injury that's healing."

"Is it on the right front hoof?" I asked.

"No, it's the back hind one," she said.

"Hmmm. I saw a picture of the right front with antibiotic salve on it right at the hoof line."

"About a month ago he had an injury there and I put ointment on it. That must be what he's showing you. Does it still bother him?" Dallas asked.

"It feels bruised, but better."

"Is he upset because he can't jump right now? It seems as if the things that used to make him happy don't anymore."

"I'll ask him if he'd like to continue jumping. Will you be all right no matter what he answers?"

"Yes," she said.

I communicated with Danny and then relayed his response.

"He says he'd rather not jump anymore," I told Dallas. "He is concerned because he wants to please you, but his hoof is not fully healed. He wants to perform to make you happy, but knows he is risking further injury right now so he is conflicted. However, there are several things that he shows me that he would like to try."

Danny sent me lots of suggestions. He showed me that he loved children and would be very happy carrying some "first timers" around in a schoolyard. He also showed me that he enjoyed the simplicity of developmentally disabled kids and would like to help. Feeling restless and full of unspent energy, he let me know he was often put away in his stall before he was ready, but that he enjoyed rolling around in the fresh hay inside the stall.

Danny had a crush on a mare that was lighter in color and he wanted to go on an easy trail ride with her. Warning that he was still concerned about potholes, he was willing to canter but galloping was still a stretch for his bruised hoof. He also said he was not often turned out to pasture with the mare he loved, and that another stallion spent more time with her. The two of them were kept apart because of concerns that they would fight. He wanted to be sure I understood that the trail ride he had in mind did not include the other stallion.

"Can you tell me anything about his life before I bought him?" Dallas asked me.

Danny was very willing to share his early life with me, sending me the feeling that he was more like property before—property that performed a function. The people who owned him were horse owners, not necessarily horse lovers, and when he turned 10 years old he was of little use to them. There was a young woman, a groom, who took care of him at his last home, and he loved her dearly. One day, she didn't show up, and no one spoke of her again. He asked me if I knew what had happened to her.

Looks like she quit the job and went away to school, I told him.

I am loved by my new mom and the woman who takes care of me now, but I first felt love with this person who brushed me, Danny told me. *There was also a trainer who came from the heart instead of the purse where I grew up, but for my owners I was a business.*

Dallas promised to try some new activities with Danny that no longer included jumping. She knew of a school for special children where he could go and she planned to introduce him to it.

"I will also try to give him some time alone with the mare he admires," she told me. "I know exactly the one he's talking about, as well as the jealous stallion. I'm sure we can arrange a trail ride with just the two of them and the mare's owner, who is a friend of mine." ☀

25

Domino Speaks

After their basic needs for food, water, and exercise are being satisfied, the number one subject domestic horses talk to me about is the bit—the bridle mouthpiece used to control and communicate with them.

Horses show me chewing on them, trying to spit them out, head tossing, and the kinds of communication they use to convey the discomfort they feel. Graphic pictures of tongue, lip, mouth, and head injuries play in my head when they talk to me, illustrating the result of the wrong kind of bit or harsher than necessary bits used by insecure or controlling riders.

According to horses, it doesn't take much of a tug on a bit to make it quite painful. That was one of the things Domino wanted to negotiate with his caretaker, Avery, who had acquired him only a few months earlier.

Avery contacted me about concerns that his black and white horse might not be getting enough exercise, since, according to some sources, horses are supposed to travel a minimum of 22 miles per day, supporting the circulation through the feet that their health depends on.

Domino was an athletic paint horse and Avery enjoyed jumping him. Driven to please and focused on doing everything just right, Domino was knotted up with tension. Having sustained some psychological damage from previous riders, it was my impression that he needed time to rest and bond before again "performing" for Avery.

I want to please him, Domino told me. *I want to do it right but sometimes I am confused by his commands. I am grateful he is so committed to my health and well-being. Just being with him is rewarding because he is so caring. This kind of human is new to me. But I can't stand this bit. Can we ride without one?*

"I'll forget trying to jump with him for a while until he heals more psychologically, even though he's fun to jump. That can wait until next summer, after we have had time to build a better relationship," Avery told me. "He does seem to play with the bit an awful lot. He has had both bosal and hackamore bits, and in the hands of an amateur rider like myself, they can be very harsh. I'm willing to give it a try, but it's very scary so please let him know it requires a lot of trust on my part."

I relayed Avery's message to his horse.

"Domino looks forward to seeing you every day and says he can count on it 'like clockwork,'" I told Avery, who confirmed his schedule was very predictable.

The results of the modified interaction were immediate and satisfying. By the following day Avery noticed dramatic changes in his horse.

"Oh my goodness! You would not *believe* the change in Domino today," he wrote me in an e-mail, then detailed the changes.

"He looked so happy to see me, as if a new level of love and bonding had taken place overnight. It was a huge change in him as he walked right over to me immediately. I could only turn him out in the pasture for about an hour before work, but when I came back after the hour he frolicked and followed me along the fence line as I approached the stables. He has never done that before. Not with that kind of animation. He must have been relieved by having his questions answered.

"I have had people talk with him before and it has not really helped our relationship as much as you have. I don't know what it is about your personality and your connection with him and what you said or how you said it, but he would hardly talk at all to the last communicator I used."

Avery had lots of follow-up questions for Domino:

"Does he want to be turned out (in a pasture) with other horses? I would be gone during that time and could not protect him. Or does he want to wait until after the temporary horses are gone for the summer? Does he have a preference as to which horses he wants to go out with and which ones to avoid?"

I'm very excited about the opportunity to be part of a herd in the wide open spaces, Domino responded, sending me the feeling that he was a jovial spirit who loved to 'kick up his heels' when allowed to bond with other horses. *I don't want to wait for this exciting opportunity. I can take care of myself. I understand Avery does not want me to get hurt like I did before, but sometimes horses play rough. Humans are more concerned about it than we are. The people that run this place know the horses that have behavior problems and they are kept separate.*

There is one jealous, aggressive gelding who is more of a problem when a certain female is turned out at the same time. He's darker brown and has a bad reputation. His attitude comes from a young, neglectful owner who seems kind of flighty and inconsistent with her visits, Domino shared with us.

I communicated more details to Avery:

"Domino shows me a black horse that is a special friend. They seem to be the same sex, so I'm going to say he's a male buddy. Domino likes young foals and fillies, so if there are any there he would love to play with them. Seems the management there is a bit overprotective when it comes to the young horses, which is keeping them from playing.

"There are also mothers of different temperaments, one in particular, very mellow, that Domino gets along well with and a pregnant mare that he likes. He doesn't need the other horses to be as energetic as he is—just being together in the pasture is enough for him."

"Does Domino understand why I must exercise him?" Avery asked.

"I'm letting him know about the exercise routine," I said. "He says he will enjoy it much more without a bit. He claims to be pretty good at exercising himself if he has the chance to run and play with others.

"None of the paints seem to be a problem for him and he shows me a special female paint horse that he likes. She's about three or four stalls down from wherever he beds down for the night. She's on the same side of the barn as he is," I relayed.

After a few days I heard from Avery again.

"I rode him today with the black blanket and brown saddle you told me he liked and only a halter. Without the bit he was the calmest I have ever seen him."

"Trusting humans has not worked well for him in the past, but he promises to work at it and asks that you give him time," I concluded. ☼

26

Donkey Dialogues

Some of my most memorable equine readings did not involve horses at all.

My first encounter with a herd of burros took place on a cold, windy winter day in Washington state. The green, gently rolling hills were covered with cedar, fir, and hemlock, as well as salal, and the lush foliage extended out 30 acres on the property owned by their caretaker, Paige. It was donkey heaven.

"They love to eat all of it," Paige said. "They're vegetarian browsers, and they'll eat shrubs, grass, sticks, and rotten wood. I can smell the aroma of fir trees on their breath sometimes when I get close."

I arrived with a bag full of carrots, and the excited animals pressed forward against the railing in the barn to get one, leaving the more shy members of the herd behind. Even the elderly ranch dog loved carrots, posturing to get a few for himself. However, I did manage to save some for our individual donkey sessions, as I was sure the animals I would be reading would be shy and reluctant, most likely needing a bit of coaxing.

Paige is one of a handful of authorities on donkeys. In 1990 she established the first abuse rescue group for them in Washington and is very knowledgeable about the animal's temperament, health, mistreatment, history, and veterinary care. She also, luckily, found her perfect assistant in Kay, who had recently bailed out of the corporate grind to fulfill her passion for animals on a horse ranch.

Bored behind a desk, Kay relinquished her hefty salary for an eight-dollar-an-hour dream job as a ranch hand, where she fell in love not only with the daily companionship of the animals but also with the ranch manager. After she and Richard were married, they spotted an ad in a newspaper looking for a couple who wanted to run a ranch and care for a herd of donkeys. Kay told me she was deeply moved by Paige's heart-centered approach to her animals, and it wasn't long before she fell in love with the donkeys too.

Paige was conscientious about the needs of her beloved herd, both physically and psychologically. She was most interested in getting more information on the peculiar behaviors of about half a dozen of these magnificent animals, so she and Kay brought each of the donkeys she wanted me to communicate with into the barn one at a time.

Tillie, the donkey Paige was most concerned about, was scheduled to go first. It took some doing to round her up and herd her into the barn. She was extremely nervous about being singled out. Not only did I get a profound sense of the jitters in Tillie, but her eyes also told the truth of her state of mind as they darted from human to exit door: She was poised to turn around and bolt at any minute.

Tillie wanted to know right away what we wanted with her, so I imagined her surrounded by a calming green energy and explained that I just wanted to talk. Pressing against a wall, I turned myself sideways so she could see me better. I also let her know I would not touch her unless she gave me permission. Her favorite handler, the kind and gentle Kay, along with Paige, were also there, which gave Tillie some comfort. While reserving judgment about why I was really there, Tillie soon opened up to me. She had a lot to say.

I'm not sure where I belong. Is this my permanent home? she asked me.

Sending me a feeling of having been moved around a lot, her message was one of being unwanted. She showed me a picture of being owned by an older man who continually grumbled about having to take care of an animal he didn't want, and of overheard conversations that let her know he wanted to get rid of her.

I felt that this lack of love and care had been her experience more than once. I also told Paige that with her previous caretakers, Tillie could not count on being fed or watered. Meals were intermittent. To make matters worse, the donkey's low self-esteem was causing the other members of the herd to bully her. As a result of moving around, she wasn't sure whether she could settle in with them and become a real member of the group.

Paige wanted me to tell Tillie that she didn't have to

perform any particular service in order to be loved and cared for.

"What does Tillie need to feel more comfortable here?" Paige asked.

The message came back loud and clear.

"Time," I said.

On a follow-up phone call two days later, these messages were validated. Paige told me that Tillie had been rescued from a farm in Ohio where an elderly man had a large herd. Their only water came from an irrigation ditch, and it wasn't good water. The man fed the animals only occasionally.

Tillie had come to Washington with her sister. Kept in a stall for six months without human contact, she was dirty but wary of grooming or brushing. Although the woman who had rescued Tillie from the Ohio farm cared about her animals, she didn't have much money and couldn't pay for a farrier to care for the donkeys' feet. With a new marriage and a new baby to attend to, the woman wasn't home much.

Clearly, Tillie wanted some reassurances that she would be staying at Paige's ranch, where a donkey could count on being well cared for.

As we stood chatting with Tillie, Paige scratched Tillie's hindquarters to relax and soothe her, but after a few minutes the donkey gave a kick, which threw a sizable rock across the room—it made a startling racket as it hit the metal barn door siding.

Paige took a step back from Tillie. "Okaaaay!" she said. "I won't scratch you there!"

"I don't think that was meant as an aggressive move," I said. "I think she was trying to get that rock out of her hoof."

I wanted to double check this later, so the next day I tuned in to Tillie telepathically from home to ask her about it. As I began to sense Tillie's feelings around the event, I felt tickled, as if her leg had been asleep and Paige's scratching had sent the blood flow back through it.

Paige had her own interpretation of the event: "I knew she wasn't trying to hurt me," she said. "Donkeys are very accurate when they kick, and if she had wanted to hurt me, she would have."

*   *   *

The next donkey I talked to was Giuseppe, a feisty young jack (a male donkey), who often initiated rough play with other members of the herd. I asked him how he had gotten the long, smooth scar on his ear, but he would only say it was nothing serious. Both Paige and Kay told me that they thought it resulted from playing roughly with another donkey friend because they bit each other's ears quite often.

One clear feeling came over me as we talked: Giuseppe was wildly crazy about Kay, who often fed, groomed, and cared for the animals. I saw him melting into a relaxed swoon when Kay began to stroke his neck and talk to him.

Giuseppe showed me that he was afraid of ropes and loud noises when, in my mind, I saw someone using him for lasso practice. It looked like they had learned the skill at his expense, hitting him with the heavy rope in the ears, eyes, muzzle, and neck before getting it right. I also felt that while he was being used for practice, he felt trapped and unable to get away. He appeared tethered to something in the middle of a ring as a young man rode around him on a horse.

"Having seen this picture, I'd expect him to be more sensitive to ropes around the head and neck area," I told the two women. "I'll tell him that will never happen here. He also wants to make sure you won't leave him tied up and go away to do other chores or errands. It seems clear to me that he was left tied up for long periods of time, and he would like some assurances."

Paige was happy for me to offer those assurances, and I relayed the message to the beautiful brown jack.

At the time, I had no idea that using donkeys for lasso practice was so prevalent, but when I talked to Paige a few days later she told me all about it.

"Horse-riding ropers used Giuseppe to practice roping cows. The donkeys are called either 'headers' or 'heelers,' which means the riders practice roping either their back feet or the head. Most of the donkeys used this way are crippled for life, especially if they're laid down and stretched out. You can easily break the animal's back," she explained.

"Why don't they just use cows?" I asked her.

"I don't know. It would make a lot more sense," she said.

Stressed out from being shuffled from place to place, Giuseppe also wanted some assurances that he would be staying put. He knew he was in a good place and wanted to know if he could actually settle in with this new herd. Paige, however, couldn't offer him those assurances.

"He belongs to a friend of mine, and I'm just taking care of him. She would give him to me if I asked her to because she travels and isn't really able to pay much attention to him right now. But I can't say exactly where he'll end up."

Finally, Giuseppe wanted to know what had happened to a young donkey, lighter in color, that he had grown attached to.

"That one followed Giuseppe everywhere and they were very close," Kay told me. "You can tell him he was only here to get weaned and then he went back to his mother."

That's why he kept looking under my body for something—it was milk! Giuseppe told me with a guffaw.

During my follow-up session with him, Giuseppe also let me know he had ultra-sensitive hearing, damaged by firecrackers and gunshots going off near where he had been penned. But he told me he enjoyed it when Kay whispered "sweet nothings" in his ears.

And Paige and Kay had a happy surprise for Giuseppe. Most likely he was going to live with his human squeeze, Kay, in the very near future. Both women were confident he would be relinquished to Kay. That boy was one lovesick donkey, infatuated with a sweet human who had loved and cared for him. I guessed that he also had a preference for blondes.

*   *   *

Star was the largest jenny (a female donkey) of the herd. She exuded confidence, stability, and security, letting me know she was the herd's matriarchal leader.

Star also sent me pictures of being with a foal. I relayed these images to Paige, who told me that Star was very attached to a youngster who spent a lot of time in her company. But I felt strongly that the picture Star sent me was more about wanting her own foal. She had a super-strong mothering instinct. Happily, there were plans to breed her.

"She's really good with babies," Paige told me.

"As far as the breeding goes, the sooner, the better, according to Star," I said.

"Can you ask Star about a cougar attack?" Paige inquired.

When I did, Star showed me a cougar jumping down on her from a tree, but she let me know her wounds had been

133

neither deep nor life-threatening. In her vision, the entire herd had ganged up on the wild cat by forming a circle. Because they kicked and bit, the cat was soon frightened away. Paige confirmed that the scratches she had found on Star were superficial and there had been no lasting damage.

To end Star's session, Paige wanted to find out if she wanted to be ridden.

I felt a bit of a backache as I checked in with Star, kind of like a backbone rubbing on a saddle.

"She wants to know if you could ride her with just a thick pad and no saddle," I said.

"Hmmm, sounds dangerous," said Paige, "but I could try a thicker pad and a lighter saddle. Maybe that would work better for her."

Finally, Star sent me a feeling of desire for a warm beverage she had seen a human drinking.

"Does someone come into the barn in the morning with a hot cup of coffee? I'm getting the sense that Star wants a sip of something hot and milky," I told Paige.

"No, I don't think so," she said, but after thinking about it she remembered that her husband often brought his mug of coffee into the barn in the early mornings.

"She'd like a sip," I said. Paige promised to relay the request to her husband.

*   *   *

When I met Star's offspring, Ritz, he was full of nervous energy. He was looking away from me across the tree-lined acreage to the other side of the ranch as I approached the gate to his half-acre pen. Sending him feelings of love and respect, I requested an audience with him. Immediately, he turned around and came to the gate where I stood. Feelings of loss, separation, anxiety, and longing swept over me and tears began to flow down my cheeks as Paige, Kay, and Richard watched.

Ritz hung his head over the gate close enough to be eye to eye with me and have a quick sniff. When I moved my face close to his head to listen carefully, he jerked his head up under my chin, leaving me with a momentary whiplash. Donkey greetings. They like to play rough.

I'm separated from the rest of the herd, he told me. *I need to be with them over the hill. I want to go over the hill.*

I relayed the message to his human caretakers and saw that he was talking about opening a gate located at the side of his pen. Through that gate lay 88 acres of wooded open space, several other donkeys, and something that interested Ritz the most: a herd of jennys.

I'll try to make that happen when our conversation is over, I promised him, turning then to his people to offer details on what he was sending me.

"I feel extremely antsy and it's as if I'm grieving over a great separation," I said. "Ritz must be a rescue animal because he tells me he has been moved around from place to place, always leaving loved ones and even offspring behind. The longing he's feeling now is about isolation from the herd that's just over the hill. Ritz is also telling me that he enjoyed a lot of attention recently and now that has evaporated."

Kay made some sense of these feelings by letting me know they had returned from a show three weeks earlier where Ritz had been the main attraction and hands-on grooming was a daily treat. Attendees admired his great stature, petted him, and offered him goodies. He loved the attention. But since the group had returned, the restless jack had been left pretty much on his own.

The only fertile male donkey on the ranch, Ritz made about $3,000 per year in sales of his very productive semen. Due to its healthy motility, he had a breeding success rate of 95 percent.

Horse breeders bought Ritz's semen to impregnate their horses and produce mules. Mules have the intelligence and power of a horse, but are much calmer in temperament than horses, who are very reactive flight animals. In addition to being less easily spooked, mules are also devoted to their handlers and are excellent workers.

"We rely on Ritz to be cooperative in our semen collection procedures, but lately he hasn't been very helpful," Paige told me. "What can we do to encourage him? We've been putting several jennys into an adjacent pen, which used to stimulate him, but that doesn't seem to be working anymore."

"Let me ask him," I said.

What's in it for me? asked Ritz.

What would you like? I asked him.

I want the gate opened and access to the back acreage, he said. *I want hands-on stroking and grooming again. And lemon cookies.*

If you got these things, would you participate in the semen collecting again? I asked.

Ritz let me know how he felt when he was in the pen getting ready for the procedure. More antsy energy.

What would make it better for you? I responded.

He projected an image of Star, showing me that he needed a calmer jenny in the adjacent pen. The seductive younger females accompanied by a protective mother figure, I thought to myself, amused. Yeah, right.

"Okay," I told Paige. "This might not make much sense in human terms since we don't generally like our parents to watch, but Ritz needs Star nearby to help him feel calmer."

"We knew he was a little different," said Kay, smiling.

Open the gate. Open the gate, Ritz kept chanting.

The three caretakers wrestled with their concern over opening the gate, which would immediately allow two mammoth jacks to enter Ritz's pen. They suspected the three would engage in food fights since Ritz had some hay left on the ground.

"It'll be all right," I told them.

So the gate was opened, the mammoths entered, went straight to the food, and began to graze. Ritz kicked up his heels and gave a loud bray to announce his displeasure. The four of us held our collective breath, hoping to avoid a donkey rumble.

I quickly sent Ritz pictures of him running over the hill and joining the other donkeys. It only took about five seconds before he moved his focus to the open gate. He trotted just outside the pen, stood for a moment and looked back to say thank you, then galloped happily over the hill. I could feel his delight for a long time after he was out of sight.

*   *   *

A session on the ranch closely connected to Ritz was one I had with Hagar, a tawny-colored fjord horse from Iceland who Paige had brought in to be a companion to Ritz. (Jacks are too aggressively territorial to be penned up together, and a different species seemed like the right solution.)

Over time, however, Ritz and Hagar would play so hard that Hagar's hip began to bother him. The vet said it had been popped out place and healed "dislocated."

136

So Hagar was taken away to rest and have some down time, and Paige asked me to check in with him.

She pointed him out to me across a half acre.

"What do you get from him?" she asked.

Hagar was standing still in the shade of a tree, but he showed me he walked with a limp.

"His problem is mechanical," I said. "It feels like a strained muscle but it will heal."

Something else was bothering Hagar.

"His stomach hurts from something white he's ingesting," I told Paige. "White pills."

Hagar was being given anti-inflammatory medication but he wasn't responding to the treatment. Soon after I left he was taken off the medicine and he felt much better. The medication was making his stomach hurt but both his stomach and his hip soon healed and he felt fine again.

*   *   *

Paige had one last donkey she wanted me to check in with. Mirage had been her very first mammoth donkey, an extra large donkey at 58-plus inches high, the one responsible for changing her mind about owning these misunderstood creatures. (The American Mammoth Jack is listed as rare by the American Livestock Breeds Conservancy.)

It was Mirage who first taught her what wonderful companions donkeys could be, dispelling all the stereotypical notions of their personalities. But Mirage had passed away, and Paige wanted to know if I could still talk to him. She handed me a photograph she had retrieved from her truck, and Mirage came through loud and clear, full of surprises.

He let me know he was the first, although at the time I didn't know what he meant.

"I thought I would never have a mammoth jack because I believed they would be too much for me," Paige said. "A donkey is much stronger and smarter than a horse and can be hard to handle. I changed my mind after seeing him and knew he needed rescuing."

Mirage claimed to be the patriarch of the herd, proud of the 10 foals he had sired, which Paige confirmed. He had suffered from an arthritic condition with swollen joints, but the main picture he sent me was one of a magnificent, strong,

137

and healthy animal. It was inspiring, along with the beautiful photo of him she showed me. No hint of illness or struggle came from him in the image he sent me, but Paige knew otherwise.

"Mirage had terrible foot problems. He was sick the whole time we had him, and his feet eventually became infected. His previous caretaker had given him a diet too high in protein, too much hot food, and inadequate foot care. He had an inflammation where the hoof separates from the bone: chronic laminitis. But he never gave up, even when covered with bedsores because of lying down—he never quit eating and drinking. When I looked at his face, I knew he wasn't ready to go and would hold on."

The magnificent patriarch wasn't very forthcoming with me, although he did admit to a bit of swelling at the joints and a problem with his feet. He transmitted a picture of strength and royalty, not Paige's reality of his long-term distress and discomfort.

*   *   *

During sessions with animals, it's nearly impossible to spend time interviewing their human companions about the accuracy of a reading, about how the information came together, or about what information they can validate. People often need some time to digest the information, and events need to unfold for predictions to come true.

An intense focus is needed to gain accurate information from an animal, but when I had a chance to interview Paige a few days later, her story confirming the accuracy of the readings, along with her personal history, unfolded as a precious memory.

Paige had been devoted to horses her entire life. "I lived, breathed, and dreamed horses. When my last one died of colic in 1985, I thought about raising miniature horses and asked about miniature donkeys, too," she said.

While shopping for miniature horses, Paige was told by a woman who had some for sale that she would trade them all in for donkeys if she had the option.

"Donkeys are much more people-oriented, interactive, and intelligent," the woman explained. "Horses are like cats, while donkeys are like dogs when it comes to temperament."

But the woman did not have any miniature donkeys for sale, so she gave Paige the name of someone who raised them. Unable to find the contact in the phone book, Paige was encouraged after seeing an article in the newspaper about the woman who raised miniature donkeys. But she still couldn't make contact, and no one at the newspaper seemed to know the woman's correct phone number.

A few months later, Paige was assigned to jury duty. The room filled up with potential jurors except for the seat right next to her. A woman who knew the miniature donkey breeder personally miraculously claimed the empty seat.

In 1993, Paige was introduced to the mammoth donkey, Mirage. Falling in love with Mirage sent her addiction to the creatures "spiraling out of control," she told me, laughing, and soon she also owned a female mammoth (Star). "I never went back to horses," she confessed.

Paige's original purpose was to sell the donkeys into happy homes. "But the bottom line is that I fall in love with all of them, and it's hard to let them go unless I find an exceptional home. I make sure they will be well cared for—I'm always looking for good animal people who will love them as much as I do," she said.

She started a donkey club, holding educational clinics and showing her animals at fairs and parades, while trying to re-educate the public on the merits of this great animal. Donkeys are known for kicking and biting, and most people don't understand either the animals or the joys of owning them.

"You need at least two donkeys, so they can play rough with each other and not with you," she advised.

While it was viable, her club rescued and placed 170 donkeys, and Paige still rescues a few when they tug at her heartstrings. To date this wonderful woman has created a spectacular life for at least 30 of these smart and funny creatures in an idyllic setting near the Olympic National Forest.

*   *   *

A year went by before I checked in with Kay to see how the herd was doing.

Guiseppe had made huge strides in his ability to trust humans and his skittishness subsided as long as Kay was nearby.

"He's here forever. He's my boy," she told me. "I'm so in love with him and he has come so far. Everyone who lives here can touch and play with him now."

Guiseppe's progress had been tested when he sustained an injury to his foot. The vet came out to take x-rays, which involved a lot of big equipment.

"The vet, his three assistants, an x-ray machine, and foot blocks were all part of the procedure," Kay remembered. "But I was right there and Guiseppe held his foot still on the blocks and did everything we asked of him. He was calm the whole time. In unfamiliar situations like this, if I leave he still panics, but his foot was cured after six weeks of babying."

I asked about Star. Kay told me that because Star was related to Ritz and he was the only fertile jack on the ranch, Star could not be bred until an appropriate jack joined the herd. In 2007 the ranch acquired a three-year-old jack who needed another season before being ready to breed. But Kay said she expected Star to finally become pregnant in the spring of 2008. Star was delighted at the news as she looked forward to realizing her dream of finally becoming a mother.

"Ritz is doing fantastically well," Kay went on. "We followed your guidelines and he loved the freedom of the 88 acres, where he could release a lot of energy. Just after you saw him in June, his libido picked up and he was bred a couple of times. We also brought in April, a beautiful seven-year-old chestnut mule, as his own private companion. Wow! He was thrilled. Buddying him up with April was a huge success."

April loved to play, and Ritz, like most donkeys, was stimulated by play and aggression.

"Ritz did much better in helping us collect his semen this year," Kay said. "I think we can attribute that to his new companion—and plenty of lemon cookies."

Hagar also benefited from Ritz and April's new friendship: The horse was given one of Ritz's offspring to raise and became completely dedicated to the youngster.

Finally, the donkey heaven caretakers were moving toward taking more natural approaches to health and foot care. Kay claimed that my communication with the animals had inspired some of these changes, including the use of Chinese herbal medicines for foot problems and a different way of hoof trimming:

"Wild horses are proven to have the best feet in the world," she explained, "and we are now using barefoot trimming methods that mimic the way wild horses' hooves are trimmed down naturally." ☀

Section V

Small Talk

*"Inasmuch as ye have done it unto one of the least
of these my brethren, ye have done it unto me."*

~ Jesus Christ, Matthew 25: 40

The anecdotes in this section appeared in *Species Link: The Journal of Interspecies Telepathic Communication* (Penelope Smith, Ed.), Issues 63 (Summer 2006) and 64 (Autumn 2006).

27

Sharing Space

With every species entitled to its space, I am cautiously charitable when it comes to cohabitating with insects that can be both helpful and dangerous. So in 2005 I made a contract with the wasps that loved to raise spring babies under the eaves of my house. Usually, I telepathically ask their "governor" to negotiate a deal with me, but this time I addressed them as a group.

"You guys can build your nests on the side of the house and we'll leave you alone, but no nests under the eaves on the front-entry side of the house. It freaks out the guests. Also, let's make a deal about no stinging me, my family, or the dog."

Only one wasp failed to get the message and began to build a nest under the front-door eaves. I sent specific messages about how the area she was building in was unsafe and let her know that I would knock the nest down before she had too much time invested in it if she failed to get the message within the next few hours. She never returned, and no one was stung. In fact, the wasps steered clear as requested.

There were about 25 wasp nests built on the side of the house that year, so the word must have gotten out. Previously, just three or four had been built there.

Unfortunately, like other insect communicators, I've had limited success with ants. When I moved back to Central California in the summer of 2007, there were a few of them who visited my new home and I opened the lines of communication with them immediately. Approaching them with respect, I let their "governess" know that I wanted no harm to come to them but that I needed them to stay outside.

"I'll give you food outside if you'll stay there," I told them. Offering a small jar of honey and some sticky hard candy outside as an incentive, along with concentrated telepathic communication that included my request for cooperation, I waited and watched.

The ants seemed to take my offers as a friendly invitation and within a few months had invaded my kitchen in numbers too great for me to cope with. I continued diplomatic talks for two months with varying degrees of success, then issued a warning.

"I'll be forced to use poisons very soon, my friends," I told them. Still they persisted in periodic invasions, while I continued with offerings of food and diplomacy.

After I was forced to use a few spritzes of ant poison, they seemed to get the message, and as the season changed from summer to winter, they also went into hibernation.

Closing the door on discussion is not an option for me these days and I keep the lines of communication open. In the past three months, two ants have been seen inside. I talked to one of them.

"What's up?" I asked him.

"We're out of honey," he said.

In the morning I found him floating in my honey-laden cup of tea and promptly deposited a mostly empty jar of honey into the garden, where the old jar lay empty. I've had no further visits.

I'm not the only one who talks to insects. In her book *The Voice of the Infinite in the Small*, Joanne Lauck writes that we need insects to survive as a species: "We cannot live on Earth for more than a few months without their recycling, harvesting, and pollinating services. Our physical survival may also depend in part on the chemical prowess of the insect kingdom. Any one of the million new insect species that scientists say await discovery and identification could provide scientific information, new products, and pharmaceuticals at great value." Remember the lowly, life-saving leech?

There was considerable discussion at my house about whether or not I should include communicating with insects in my book since it's pretty "far out." A few agents considering representing this book felt it would have a better chance with publishers if I cut out the section altogether. But what can I say? I'm one of those people destined to make deep connections with other species and pass along their healing gifts while working on their behalf. Sometimes it feels as if I'm a telephone repairperson perched on a high pole on a wintry night with blowing snow coming at me as I solder tiny wires together between humanity and other species. But like Joanne

Lauck, I also have an abiding interest in the healing potential inherent in our relationship with all life.

I'll make my case *and* hedge my bets. By offering many professional voices on this subject who relay their experiences, I expect to appear a lot saner.

Besides, the stories are real, they're fascinating, and they offer a toxic-free way to relocate bugs while honoring their place in the universal scheme of things.

That's my rationale and I'm sticking to it. ☀

28

Ant-ipathy

Little black ants that once resided outside had moved into animal communicator Lyn Benedict's garage in a big way. Out of the anthills they'd once occupied just outside her six-car garage, hauling sand in a grain at a time, they built homes on the concrete floor. Since half of the garage is heated and carpeted for Lyn's dog training business, she knew the ants would be a problem in that location. With a history of successfully moving other critters, she set out to relocate the ants through empathetic communication channels.

"I asked the ants to leave and explained that outside the door was fine but inside was not okay with me. I told them that I was allowing ants in the greenhouse beds, but not in the house or garage," she writes.

Because there was no food in the garage, Lyn knew the ants were just looking for a warm, dry place and she had vowed several years before not to use chemicals on bugs. Posing her request, she asked for a response in 24 hours.

"The next day nothing changed and I asked them again to please move outside but I didn't feel they were listening or responding," she says.

Lyn's previous successes using communication included moving wasps that lived over the garage door and asking the rabbits to stay out of the yard because they were a source of fleas. Both of these creatures responded cooperatively. But the ants didn't seem to be getting the message.

"The next day, I asked one more time. This time I told the ants I would have to use ant poison if they didn't move by the time we went on our two-week vacation at the end of the week. Still nothing changed with the ants in the garage and I felt ill at the thought of having to do something to get rid of the ants.

"I sat down on the floor in the garage and asked to talk to the Ant Diva (Oversoul, or Lead Spirit), explaining what the situation was again," she recalls. "This time she appeared to me and listened but said nothing. These ants didn't seem to feel that I had any right to be asking them to move. I knew they'd been there first, but I was hoping we could share our acre of land. I was left thinking that I would have to use ant poison in three days just before we left on our trip."

The sight that greeted Lyn the next morning in the garage shocked her.

"Even from a distance, I could see that the piles of sand were moving. When I got close, they were roiling in activity. There were huge half-black, half-red ants there now. I felt sick to my stomach and became very angry, so I left and avoided that part of the garage all day. I figured that more were moving in instead of leaving as I had hoped. I was very sad.

"The next day I went out and approached the ant colony cautiously. Before I got close, I knew something was amiss. I could see no movement. As I got closer, I saw little dead black ants. Dismayed, I saw they were dead both inside and outside the garage, and that's not what I wanted. There were a few big black and red ants walking around with white things in their mouths so I figured they were moving into the homes where the little black ants had lived. That, too, was depressing. We would leave in a couple of days and I would have to use the poison."

Upset about the dead black ants, Lyn sat down and cried again, calling on the Ant Diva. This time she responded directly to Lyn's emotional request.

"I also asked the black ants to leave and they refused me, too," said the Ant Diva. "So I consulted the Great Spirit who said I was to send in troops to take out the black ants. Spirit said we must honor your request at all costs. The red and black ants are carrying away black ant larvae. The ants are gone and they will not be back."

Lyn felt sorrowful that some of the ants had to die but the Ant Diva told her it was their choice.

"The ants were asked many times and each time they refused. Do not feel sorrowful," she said.

The following day was the last day before Lyn left on vacation. With no evidence of remaining ants around the sand piles, she decided to vacuum in order to clearly detect whether they had completely relocated when she got back a few weeks later.

"When we returned home, there were no traces of sand in the garage," Lyn writes. "The rest of that summer, I watched closely. Just five feet outside the door, there was a lot of ant activity, but none inside the garage. Even the following summer, the ants abided by the agreement, and I consciously sent them gratitude for listening and taking the matter into 'their own hands' so that I didn't have to resort to using poison. It was a great lesson for me in how the Universe sees the act of asking."

*   *   *

Penelope Smith also made a deal with a group of ants. Her new concrete and stucco house, completed in 1997 after a forest fire destroyed her previous redwood home, was bermed into the hillside.

"In the first rainy season, the ants came marching in, naturally, since the house was partially in the ground right alongside their houses, too. They were seeking shelter and showed me that their burrows were full of water from the heavy rains," she writes in her publication, *Species Link*.

"I didn't mind them being in the house, but I did mind them raiding the cupboard and being all over the counters. I even found them in the freezer. I sealed up my food in containers and told them we could cohabit peacefully, but with hundreds of them all over my food preparing areas, it was difficult not to kill them and hard to operate around them. I advised them to seek higher ground outside and worked out with them where their colony would do best without getting flooded out. I also offered them food outside until they could recover from the flooding."

In the meantime, while the ants were rebuilding their homes, Penelope surrounded the counters and cupboards with diatomaceous earth, a powdery substance that dries up insect bodies but is non-toxic to other animals.

"I warned the ants that the diatomaceous earth was there, and while a few walked through the white powder and dried up, they quickly sent word to the rest of the colony, and no one else crossed the diatomaceous line. The ants found the cat food the greatest attraction, so I put the cat food dish in a shallow bowl filled with water, creating a moat that the ants couldn't cross," she recounts.

"After the ants adjusted to their new homes on flood-free ground over a few seasons, they still crossed through the house in their established routes on the floor but never again

150

went into the food or on the counters or kitchen area. They stayed on the floor and even stopped going to the cat food. I enjoyed watching them appear and disappear into the cracks. We happily cohabitated on Mother Earth together," she writes.

Penelope teaches telepaths how to deepen the connection between themselves and the animal kingdom, thereby honing their skills to new levels of accuracy. She says for the communication to be most effective it's essential to understand an animal's viewpoint and then to work out a mutually beneficial arrangement. ☀

*   *   *

Lyn Benedict • wolftalker@theglobal.net

Penelope Smith • www.animaltalk.net

29

Manhattan's Oldest Residents

The effectiveness of interspecies communication is sometimes so dramatic it just can't be denied. Donna Lozito's story illustrates that. She's been doing animal communication work for about a decade and is also a designer, which offered one of her clients a bonus when they employed her: It saved them the cost of an exterminator.

The job involved construction of the entire 48th floor of one of New York City's skyscrapers in which the employees had no choice but to remain in temporary workstations during construction.

"The insects, rodents, and various other species love the homes they have so cleverly constructed in the walls and between the floors of these towers that line the skies of New York," Donna writes. "One day this spring, I was called to see how the roaches (the large ones that fly) were dropping out of the ceiling onto people and even crawling inside the clothes of some of the employees. The employees demanded that I call an exterminator. They had already killed one of the bugs, who I could see lay crushed on the floor.

"The women were hysterical and even the men, in their style, were equally hysterical. I told them I would not call an exterminator but that I would like to ask the roaches to leave. The looks from the group were priceless. This particular group, clearly representing mainstream corporate America, gasped at the thought of speaking with a roach."

Many interspecies communicators report that the most successful insect relocations involve offering an alternative living situation, as well as graphically transmitting what will happen should the insects decide to stay put. Donna followed this guideline:

"I proceeded to explain to the roaches that if they did not leave the area there would be more deaths like the roach who had already been crushed," she writes. "I explained that if they did not leave, the exterminator would come and the entire floor would be fumigated. They clearly understood and agreed to go."

"The construction workers and employees thought that I should be committed as insane for this act but they were desperate. They had no choice but to wait and see if this communication had done any good. Since it was Friday afternoon, even if I had agreed to an exterminator it would have taken at least until Monday for one to come. I was sure that our roaches understood my message and they would not return at least for a while.

"To the amazement of the employees, the bugs did not return for the rest of the week. At least they did not interfere with the humans who invaded their space. Then on the following Friday, an employee summoned me to the area again, but this time the request went like this: 'Donna, could you please talk to the roaches again. One fell from the ceiling and we would like them to leave.' I could feel their presence in the partially opened ceiling.

"When I contacted the roaches, I said, 'If you don't leave, this group will make me call an exterminator and it will be unpleasant for us all.' I got an angry reply. 'Where do you want us to go?' I told them to go up or go down but to get off this floor, at least until the work was complete.

"I explained to the workers that the roaches were angry, and that these bugs had been living peacefully in this building for a long time and all of a sudden we had invaded their space and their lives. I explained that the roaches felt they had just as much right to be in between the floor as the people had to be on that floor, if not more.

"As I conversed further with the roaches, the leader of the group said that it really was an accident this time. His mate had been walking along the grid and slipped and fell to his death. They agreed again to leave the premises temporarily. They kept their agreement.

"We have not seen a roach since. We had reports that people saw our insect friends on the 47th and 49th floors in the weeks following, and I have since communicated that for a while they would have to be very careful where they stepped. They agreed and appreciated the warnings.

"I am pleased that part of corporate America has experienced the level at which other species can communicate," Donna concludes. "The employees of this particular firm may not have complete acceptance of what other beings have to offer us but they certainly have something new in their experience of animal communication work."

As Penelope Smith, a pioneer in the field and editor of *Species Link*, wrote in response to Donna's account: "The ripples from our sacred small-creature connection spread and people awaken." ☀

*   *   *

Donna Lozio • donna@animalchatroom.com

30

Literal Critters

Animals and insects are very literal creatures, so an interspecies communicator has to be careful how messages are worded.

The large field behind professional animal communicator Marilyn Tokach's home is a place where rabbits, field mice, and ground squirrels live, and talking to them proved this point.

"I was determined not to use chemical animal deterrents or pesticides, since my goal was a harvest of organic veggies," she writes, "so I telepathically contacted my herbivorous neighbors and offered the animals one-half of the garden's harvest in exchange for no disturbance of buds, leaves or plant roots."

As the plants sprouted and grew, the tomatoes were transformed from small green globes, to yellow, and then to orange. Marilyn could hardly wait for the fruits of her labor to end up on the dinner table.

"On the day I felt the first tomato would surely be ripe, I planned a salad for lunch. As I walked toward the garden, I anticipated the juicy sweet-tart taste of the tomato I nurtured to ripeness.

"There it was: one half of a beautifully ripe red tomato still attached to the vine. It seems the fruit had been sheared with my half dangling, waiting to be picked. The tomato was divided evenly from top to bottom, stem intact. The wild ones had quite literally honored our agreement!"

Marilyn connected once again with the animals, thanking them for honoring her request and leaving her half on the vine. But this time, she revised her bargain.

"Let's share our bounty a different way," she told them. "In whole parts—one for you and one for me."

She reports, "As the vegetables continued to ripen, I always found whole, ripe veggies hanging on the plants. None rotted on the ground and none had insect holes or rodent nibbles.

"Now I am careful to identify and clearly communicate my desires," she says. ☀

*   *   *

Marilyn Tokach • www.Pure-Spirit.com

31

Crickets' Agreement

"I like insects and love talking to them," says animal healer and communicator Elizabeth Severino.

"My favorite experience happened in 1987 when I moved to a home in Cherry Hill, New Jersey," she writes. "I quickly realized that the adjoining garage and house were overrun with crickets. At times dozens of them were visible, suggesting the unseen presence of hundreds.

"Although I personally admire the ease with which crickets jump and the joy with which they congregate, I did not want dozens of crickets leaping about in my home, frightening my daughter and startling me. I also did not want my Oriental rugs or clothing eaten or damaged by the crickets. I did acknowledge their right to a good life.

"Late one afternoon, just before the crickets would normally begin singing, I spoke to them. I stood in the middle of my home and expanded my telepathic net to embrace the entire house, as I energetically addressed all the crickets at the same time.

"I told them I would always provide suitable food and water in the garage behind the cabinets that are around the walls and they could place themselves there when it was time for them to be invisible to me. I told them they could have access to my home in the event they wanted to run around in a larger space, but explained that I never wanted to see or hear them. I also asked them not to eat anything inside my home.

"I made it clear that when I was home, they were to be silent and out of sight. I told the crickets that if necessary, in the event we were working in the garage, they were to temporarily leave the property altogether. If I saw any of them, they needed to understand that I would take that as a request for them to leave their body form. I would then facilitate their release to another dimension. They agreed instantly.

"Many months went by during which this 'contract' was

perfectly honored. Then, one night, I wasn't feeling well. In the middle of the night, I went downstairs with the intent to heat up some milk to help induce restful sleep. I flipped on the light and was very startled to find the entire kitchen full of crickets! They let out a telepathic yell of surprise and scurried madly to the sides of the room and into adjacent rooms.

"'What happened to our understanding?' I demanded.

"'You didn't give us enough time to move away!' they wailed.

"We instantly all co-created the mutual understanding that in the future, if I were to go downstairs in the middle of the night, I needed to send the thought, 'I'm about to turn the light on.' Then I would wait long enough to give them time to get completely out of sight.

"Although house sitters and visitors to my home in my absence saw and heard the crickets, this arrangement continued to work perfectly until I sold the house in 2002," Elizabeth concludes. ☼

* * *

Elizabeth Severino • www.elizabethseverino.com

32

Tiny Vampires

When Sheila Waligora moved to Botucatu, Brazil, she had a hard time sleeping. The mosquitoes were a hungry and noisy group, biting and buzzing around her head while she attempted to get a little shuteye. Allergies to chemical products made applying a repellent impossible, so to get some relief from the tiny vampires she took another tack.

"I had just read Joanne Lauck's book, *The Voice of the Infinite in the Small,* and I made a firm decision to talk to the mosquitoes and make a gentle agreement with them," she writes. "So at the end of the day, I would sit outside in my hammock, and let the mosquitoes have a blood meal on me. I recognized that they needed to eat as much as I did, so I also started offering them sugar from fruit, which I would put in various places in the house.

With great respect, she asked them to leave her alone at night so she could sleep, and as she began to communicate with them, her love for them grew, along with a realization that they were important in the scheme of things.

"From that time on, they respected my wish and never again bothered me," Sheila says. "I always tell this story during animal communication talks and courses and many people then try to communicate with mosquitoes and they've had positive results. They're amazed they can talk to the mosquitoes instead of using poison, which pollutes themselves and the environment."

The mosquito encounter taught Sheila that making agreements with other species requires genuine respect and an acknowledgment of the very important role they play in the web of life. These are critical to successful negotiations. ❋

*   *   *

Sheila Waligora • www.comunicacaoentreespecies.com.br

33

The Beetles

Beetles that looked like ladybugs lived in professional animal communicator and canine behavior specialist Karla McCoy's house all winter, but usually they disappeared after fall. At first, she looked at them as a nuisance and was tired of wiping them off counters or water bottles. Then one day, she decided to give it up and live peacefully with them in the house.

"I asked my husband how many he was seeing and he said one or two here and there, but I was seeing five or six a day. They were crawling on windows or cabinets when I decided to just let them be," she writes.

Weeks went by and one day Karla realized they were gone!

"I accepted them and they left!" she says. "Then I was sad to see them go. I had learned to feel and to appreciate their presence and sometimes during those early spring days I actually found myself smiling at their behavior."

A few weeks later, a thick group of ants arrived. Escorting about a dozen of them outside several times a day, she soon remembered the experience with the beetles and decided if the ants wanted to live in her house, she would make peace with that too.

"I have only seen one or two ants in the house since then," Karla writes. "As with the beetles, I've grown used to their presence and am appreciating them if they choose to live in my home."

When I asked her about her relationship with the beetles a year later she said, "There are no beetles in my house this year. I have to say, I do miss their sparkling little bodies of life." ☀

*   *   *

Karla McCoy • www.AnimalTell.com

34

Fire Ants and Banana Spiders

The first morning Diane Samsel moved from Cincinnati to a Charleston, South Carolina, beach, she found the kitchen counter covered with tiny little ants.

"They didn't listen to me when I asked them to leave," writes the interspecies communicator, "so I took a paper towel and gently began to wipe them away. In a flash, ants covered my hand and, on command, they bit me all at the same time. That was my painful introduction to fire ants!"

Diane next decided to contact the queen.

"I was taken aback by her rage, but I managed to get into a long and educational conversation with her. Her main complaint was about humans who have killed her repeatedly. She didn't understand why this had to be," she says.

"I showed her how horribly painful her sting was, and told her we couldn't live with that. We negotiated a truce. I agreed to dump a bag of outdated Power Paws™ powdered supplement under the steps of our house, and she agreed to move her nest to pine straw. She built many tunnels under the Power Paws and ate from the pile for about nine months.

"I didn't know where the nest had been moved, but she kept her end of the bargain by staying out of the kitchen and the house," Diane reports. "She put a tunnel outside under the flowerpots because we're having a drought and that's where there's water. That's okay with me. I haven't been bitten since we declared a truce."

Diane also tells a story about another beach-dwelling insect she has grown to admire in her new home.

"I love the energy of the golden orb spider. They're called banana spiders because their bodies are long and yellow. They can grow to the size of an outstretched human hand and they build wonderful webs. By July, they form a necklace around our cottage, which is on 12-foot stilts because of the flood plain. The banana spiders suspend their webs in a circle around our stilts and below our eaves. I find them to be exquisite souls. One grew under the eaves right by our front door and the UPS woman almost refused to deliver to us because of her!

"On Dewees Island, we love our banana spiders and have an unofficial spider-growing contest to see which house gets the biggest spider," Diane says. "I look forward to a world where we can live in harmony with big spiders, snakes, and alligators, as we do here on Dewees Island." ☀

* * *

Diane Samsel • www.powerpaws.com

35

Reiki Mouster and Tarantula Teacher

Soon after Winterhawk's cat, Marcel, the Reiki Mouster, went to heaven, houseflies began to visit both Winterhawk and her partner. Sometimes a fly was especially attentive, alighting on their hearts or other chakras, tickling them with a tingling sensation. During these visits, they began to experience the same Reiki bliss as previously transmitted by Marcel. (Reiki—literally meaning "spiritually guided life force energy"—is a Japanese technique for stress reduction and relaxation that also promotes healing.)

"Marcel received Reiki attunement through his beloved friend and fan, animal communicator and Reiki Master Dr. Jeri Ryan. Marcel had a way of sending Reiki that would put my partner and me into the deepest theta wavelengths for long, lovely times," Winterhawk writes.

When the flies alighted and offered their healing work, putting Winterhawk into a blissful state, she happily began to ask one fly, "Is that you, Mouster?" And the conversations began.

"The fly would zip from one of us to the other, performing his special, loving magic," Winterhawk writes. "We have received attunements and transmissions, healings and joy from Marcel's company in these sessions. I bless these willing little messengers and our dear Reiki Mouster."

Many years into the intentional practice of opening ears, eyes, and hearts, Winterhawk says she is gratefully humbled by each lightning-strike crack in her universe, each encounter forged purposefully by pure love.

"I'm indebted to these little insect teachers," she says. "Their unexpected visits and brilliant rays of wisdom, compassion, and humor have tickled me, brought me to the tearful knees of my own fear and arrogance, and helped to heal our connection. One special encounter revealed how an unexpected housemate became a medicine teacher.

"During the first evening back in a country-like setting

after many city years," she writes, "I felt carried by the land and the deep, old eucalyptus fragrance to sit with the trees under the stars. Facing my low beach chair toward the hilly slope full of deer trails, tall grasses, and wonderful trees, I sent out a mental call: 'Wouldn't it be lovely to discover a little fawn or raccoon?'

"I became aware of a sensation that I was not alone, experienced as a clear, cool feeling and a large silvery energy field," Winterhawk remembers.

"Out of the darkness, just a yard away, strode a large tarantula, moving quite purposefully and stopping in front of me, as if she had been called! I realized later how much she wanted contact. Her own needs evaded me in my surprise, and I tried to be cordial, though I was truly unprepared. We chatted a bit, and then I rather hurriedly excused myself to go inside. I saw her walk toward our basement and felt some trepidation about more surprise encounters."

This initial meeting with the tarantula was to begin a long relationship between the spider messenger and Winterhawk.

Mid-dreamtime one night, Winterhawk's partner sprang out of bed, crying, "There's a spider on the bed!"

"Out of sleepy habit, I jumped up, too," Winterhawk says. "But after an unsuccessful search, it dawned on me to ask, 'What kind of spider?'"

"Black and verrryyy big," came her mate's wide-eyed reply. "It was on top of your chest!"

Winterhawk understood then and laughed.

"'Oh, it's Nari, my dreamtime spider,'" Winterhawk explained to her partner. "'You became aware of her in your sleep,' I told her. She could really put out the vibes, this spider woman!"

Winterhawk recounts:

"After that, Nari became a frequent visitor in dreams and vision. She first appeared in the form of a very dark-skinned Aboriginal woman. That's when I learned that the eucalyptus is the 'dreaming tree' in Australia. Nari seems to shape-shift from tree to woman to spider, whatever serves her to teach and to travel. She's worked with many women the world over, teaching ancient women's medicine ways of seeing and being.

"Nari is a no-nonsense medicine teacher, and stands behind me. I feel her calling us back to work together.

"Still, her return brings some trepidation. She is pure raw power, cutting to the quick without a word in her teaching. I am more ready now, and I thank her, but I hope Nari's tarantula spider form found another good friend who appreciated her beauty and gifts, and might have been more able to touch her than I was.

"I know she would have been a fast friend physically had I been able to manage that." ✸

*   *   *

Winterhawk • http://home.earthlink.net/winterhawkac

36

Termites Take a Hike

x x x x x x x x

Insects flying around the window caught animal communicator Brenda Cunliffe's eye and she walked over to see what it was.

"I noticed hundreds of the same little flying creatures there and I thought they might be some kind of flying ant," she writes.

"I called my family in to look at them and my daughter informed me that she had seen some of the same insects down in her room too," Brenda remembers. "My husband took one look at the window case and determined that we didn't have flying ants; we had termites and lots of them! As he promptly looked up the number of an exterminator in the phone book, I asked him to give me a chance to talk with the termites and ask them to move on instead. He agreed, but had already made an appointment for the exterminator to come to our house two days later because he wanted them gone one way or the other."

Brenda talked with the termites and explained that they would have to move their colony, showing them the possibility of relocating to the woods behind her house.

"I told them that I was giving them a warning and if they didn't heed my words they would be killed," Brenda says.

"Picturing long, narrow tunnels that went far below the ground where the rest of their families and colonies lived, I showed them an image of a human drilling holes in the foundation of our house and the surface of the ground. I telepathically transmitted the loud noise and vibration of the drill, and a thin white liquid poison pouring down the tunnels drowning or suffocating any termites in the path.

"For those lucky enough to have avoided the cascade of poison, their fate was still sealed, as the liquid would seep into the ground around the tunnels, tainting the earth and killing them as their feet made contact. I explained that if any termites miraculously made it to the top of the tunnel, they would find the tunnel blocked with a thick layer of poisonous white foam that would destroy them as they tried to wade through it.

"I concluded my communication by transmitting their two options again: move to the woods or suffer a terrible, chemically induced death.

"Two days later, my husband escorted the exterminator to the area of the house where the termites had been seen," Brenda writes. "Together they checked the upstairs and downstairs. The exterminator found some termite damage to our windowsills and hardwood floors but did not find a single termite!" ☀

* * *

Brenda Cunliffe • www.commiskey.biz

37

Front Porch Buzz

The front porch at Karen Kober's house was a place where she wanted to be able to sit after supper and watch the beautiful Pennsylvania sun set just over the ridge. But many springs, summers, and autumns passed by because of bugs swarming at that time of day, while she and her dog Foxx stayed inside.

"My dreams of enjoying this special time of day had been shattered like glass in the evening breeze as a horde of black wings swooped down from the nearby crab apple tree. Swarming black bugs, larger than gnats, darted at my face," she writes in her article, "Paper Wings," in *Species Link*.

"I could feel their paper wings as they painfully bit my flesh. I closed my eyes, tightened my mouth, and wildly flung my hands about my face, as I attempted to make it back into the house quickly."

As she stood up to head for the door, Karen remembered that the instructor from an animal communication workshop had said that a Soul Leader from any group of species would listen to her request and respond.

"I sat back down, lamenting, 'Well, here goes nothing.' With bugs biting at my face, I found it difficult to send a telepathic message to the Soul Leader of this black winged invasion," she recalls.

"Finally, I managed to introduce myself. I gave the black bugs love and blessings, and then asked the Soul Leader to take everyone back to the flowering tree to enjoy the blossoms and leave Foxx and me to enjoy the porch.

"In a nanosecond, the bugs turned like a school of fish and went back into the crab apple tree," she wrote.

"It works, it works!" she exclaimed to herself with hands clenched in victory.

"Many years have passed," she writes. "Foxx and I have shared countless evenings talking on the front porch.

"We watch the yellow, pink, and orange sunsets change

color over the ridge without a black bug in sight," she concludes. ☼

*   *   *

Karen Kober • www.foxx.funn.net

38

Mr. Slug and Other Wild Friends

"My early life, before animal communication, began with a typical view of insects: creepy, crawly, dangerous, irritating little beings. But something inside me saw quite a different picture," writes Morgine Jurdan. "In science class, when instructed to crack off the shell of a snail, I refused to do so. I had no desire to kill the small harmless creature."

Her perspective turned around "in the blink of an eye" during her first animal communication class. Morgine was instructed to spend some quiet time with an animal friend as a homework assignment, noticing what she felt and observed.

"I had no animal companion with me so I was instructed to go out in Nature and 'be with' whatever showed up first. To my great dismay, a slug appeared. I was less than excited, but I decided to try my skills with the little slug," she writes.

"After sitting with the slug for a while, to my surprise, the little being began to ask me questions.

"It wanted to know if I could tell what kind of food I was eating when I closed my eyes! It asked me if I could tell what clothes I was wearing, if I was inside or outside, and what kind of building I was in. It asked me if I could feel the vibrations in the ground or in the air, describe the texture of the air, discriminate between fragrances, and see without using my eyes by using my inner senses to detect energies.

"After about a half hour, I came to realize how limited I was in using the magnificent body in which I live every day. Here was a little creature that I seldom paid attention to who was so alive and who dramatically changed the way I experienced my world!

"I began to take the time to taste and smell my food, feel my clothes, and experience the energies of my everyday surroundings. My little friend, a blessed slug, began me on a lifetime journey of discovering more of who I am. After 13 years and over 2,000 animal consultations and conversations, the experience with the slug remains among my favorite and most enlightening experiences."

Another memorable insect communication Morgine experienced was through a woman she met in a class. The woman shared with friends that ants had covered her patio and deck for the third spring in a row. The first year she and her husband left them alone and stayed inside. The second year they tried natural remedies but the ants remained. Year number three, they were on the verge of using chemicals to kill the ants when Morgine told her the ants might have a message for her.

"Call for a consultation if you're interested," she told her classmate, who contacted her soon after.

"The ants transmitted a message for her and her husband that brought them both to tears," Morgine writes. "It was about their relationship and some changes they needed to make in order to renew the love they had for each other. The couple ended up going outside and thanking the ants after our consultation. The next day, the ants were gone and were not seen again during the rest of that 10-week class," Morgine says.

Even for animal communicators, it sometimes takes repeated behaviors for critters to get our attention. For Morgine, it was a group of mice who persisted until she opened her communication channel to receive their message.

"I had a mouse in my 'catch them alive' trap every day for a week when I finally sat down and asked the mice what they wanted me to know. The message I received was about slowing down; not trying to do too many things at once. Once I got the message, the traps were empty," she says.

Another message came to her from a normally dangerous spider. Morgine received a dramatic bite from a few brown recluse spiders that bit her four times in five years. Their bite is nasty, leaves a brown spot bigger than a hand at the site, and can be fatal for some people.

"By the fourth bite, I realized the spiders must be trying to tell me something," she writes. "The recluse spiders bit me on the same place on my inner thigh. I asked Spirit for the message the spider was attempting to share with me. It was about some energetic clearing I needed to do in the area of my female organs and I followed the spider's advice about how to accomplish this clearing. After that, decades of feminine issues, including yeast infections, went away for good."

When tilling and planting a garden, Morgine also communicated with insects and other wild creatures according to the methods she read about in a breakthrough book that many animal communicators have used.

"I co-created a garden with Nature using some processes I learned in the book *Behaving As If the God in All Life Mattered*, by Machaelle Small Wright," Morgine writes. "Putting a lot of love into the garden every time I planted, cleaned, or watered, I talked with the insects and deer who slept 20 feet away several nights each week. I carefully placed a ribbon around the circular garden and the deer never entered. Rarely were there any detrimental insects inside this circle, although they thrived elsewhere in my yard.

"I believe the world I live in is created with balance in mind. When something is out of balance, actions go into motion to restore it," Morgine says. "Insects will give up their lives trying to relay these messages, but unfortunately, we often kill the messenger. When we clear-cut a forest for example, often the first things to grow back are plants with stickers or thorns, like blackberries. They protect the land until more things can grow back and become strong. In our homes, sometimes we have ants, termites, flies, or mice. They are merely coming to let us know something is out of balance in our lives.

"Nowadays when a fly lands on my computer screen while I'm working, I stop and ask, 'What's your message?'" she says with a laugh.

"Learning to experience the sacred in all of life can bring us back to our roots and our connection to Nature, and it might even save our lives. It could mean avoiding destroying something that could keep us from extinction," Morgine advises. ☀

*　　*　　*

Morgine Jurdan • www.communicationswithlove.com

Section VI

Stars To Steer By

*"The inner voice speaks not in words but
in the wordless language of the heart."*

~ Osho Zen Tarot

39

The Limits of Telepathy

Communication of any kind is tricky, but telepathic messages can be quite ambiguous: I get pictures, smells, feelings, visions, pains in the body, and all sorts of sense-related 'cues.' Then it's up to the client and me to interpret this information. We're often playing a form of charades.

During a psychic reading a universe of information opens up and the reader has to choose a particular direction. Home, finances, health, relationships, past lives, and many other areas of life can be attuned to, and, without a direction or specific questions, the reader has to make choices or data can come through in general terms. When a new client begins a session with the admonition, "Okay, go ahead," I know we could be on the same page or not depending on my choice of the road we'll travel.

Animals answer questions but rarely volunteer a lot of information without inquiry. This situation is aptly illustrated by a client I'll call Betty, who contacted me via e-mail. As this e-mail session shows, I sometimes rely on an animal's caretaker to help interpret some of the pictures I get and to point me in a direction by asking particular questions.

In her first correspondence, Betty asked simply, "Can you connect with animals that have passed on?"

"Yes Betty, I can. Thanks for asking. If you want to proceed, please e-mail a picture of your pet," I replied.

"I appreciate your response," she answered. "I have attached a picture. I hope you can help me."

Crystal, Betty's beautiful husky, had one brown eye and one blue. She was a striking animal and I was dazzled by her image. Her body appeared transparent, the first clue that an animal has passed on to the other side.

"What a wonderful animal Crystal is and was," I wrote Betty in my e-mail response. "She first told me she was a 'constant companion.' I take that to mean she was with you all of the time, or that you took her everywhere you went.

"I also saw a harness, just like the kind one uses for a seeing-eye dog. I don't know if this is a sign that she was in service, felt like she was of service to you, or was an actual seeing-eye dog.

"She showed me a red rubber ball also, positioned right between her front legs as she lay there, in the same pose as in the picture you sent."

Crystal seemed to be an "angel dog" who had a divine appointment with Betty. Thoughts and pictures kept coming that told me service was the "theme" of her life. I told Betty that her dog felt very useful, purposeful, and well-loved. She had shown me pictures of being admired for her beauty as the two of them took walks around the neighborhood. I felt there was some teasing about it by Betty, and I asked her if she joked that Crystal was vain.

"I am having a harder time getting her to show me the end of her life, since she sees herself as the magnificent creature in the photo. But there was a feeling of an impact injury," I said.

"Crystal showed me that she liked carrots, and said you conscientiously fed her a very healthy diet.

"One of her duties was guard duty, mostly at night as you slept. She was very alert at the foot of the bed. But she does not show me sleeping on the bed. She says she wasn't allowed on the furniture, but that she had her own designated spaces. She spent most of her time on the floor, watching out for you and looking outside, and was a great lover of the outdoors.

"Crystal says a male used to throw her something in the air. She was good at catching it. Could it be popcorn? It was something edible, since Crystal was lying down in the living room while he shared a treat as well as playing catch."

I continued with the reading as the pictures flowed.

"Crystal says she had a cat friend, a very young kitten when they first met.

"As I scan Crystal's body, I feel a problem in the kidneys or liver area, and this may have been her ultimate problem. She was good at masking her pain, but doing so became harder and harder.

"She still visits you, and says there's another dog that has taken her place, younger and less experienced, and perhaps in training.

"Let me know if any of this sounds like I am tuning in to

the right animal. She sure was and is grand. There is a great feeling of pride when I tune in to her. She was truly a blessing, and it must have been hard to let her go. I know you had a very special bond, and she is also aware of it. She sends her love and a lick."

Betty's response was short and to the point.

"I appreciate your effort, but that had to have been another dog," she wrote. "I got my dog very abused and she was in no way a service dog. It took me a long time to help her past the abuse, several years. She was beaten and starved, and was about to have puppies when I got her. She also never played.

"My Crystal also did not have a kidney or liver problem. I have been wondering if she was still on the other plane or reincarnated. Thanks for trying. My dog passed years ago, and I wondered how long they stick around."

I wanted to investigate this further and find out how the reading could be so inaccurate, so I continued questioning Betty about the particular pictures I had been given. I also wanted to explain some of the specific reasons Crystal might not share information Betty expected.

"Dogs often do not wish to revisit their abusive situations," I wrote. "Instead they like to dwell on the happy times they had with the person asking about them. Once they pass over, they are all about love, and it's tough to get them to show you that they were once starved and abused.

"The rubber ball may have been an invitation to play with her memory now, or showing you that she can play more easily now that she's out of a body that was so badly treated.

"The picture of the liver or kidney trouble could be a problem in the same general area of her body, since I am not especially good at anatomy. This might seem like a rationalization, but I don't know of a time when I have been as far off as you indicate. While some pet psychics are medical intuitives and have an extensive knowledge of the canine body, my area of expertise is in the emotional arena. Crystal was a happy dog at the end of her life.

"She might not be sending me pictures of misery suffered years before; it's just not in their nature, especially once they are on the other side.

"As a client, it's important to let your psychic know what you want to find out. Your initial inquiry included only one question: Can I tune into animals that have passed? You indicate here that you wanted to know if she had reincarnated.

It would have been appropriate to ask that question to get the energy flowing and to open up the lines of communication.

"Dogs with humans who are very private will not reveal things they think their human would not like them to reveal, even the most mundane things—they become private too. They are very honorable creatures.

"Your response tells me everything you picked out that you felt was incorrect, but does not address so many other areas of the reading. Does this mean:

1. You do not feel she was of service to you in any way?
2. She rarely went anywhere with you?
3. You did not speak of her physical beauty?
4. She was never useful, or well-loved?
5. You were not especially careful about her diet?
6. She was allowed on the furniture and slept on your bed?
7. You did not regularly walk together for exercise?
8. Others did not admire her?
9. You do not have another dog now that is younger, or did not get another younger dog after she passed?
10. How did she ultimately pass?

"I would love to get the answers to these questions. I am always interested in readings in which clients feel I have not tapped into the right animal since I wish to hone my skills and strive to understand the true nature of telepathic communication."

I closed by thanking Betty for her help.

She wrote back with further feedback on the seemingly off-the-mark session.

"I do believe that dogs reincarnate and that you may have tuned into an earlier life of hers, which I guess made me wonder if she did not remember her life with me. Isn't that possible?

"I took her with me often. She was quite beautiful and several people made that comment. She was very useful in that she made my heart happy, and the doctor made me put her on a healthy diet right away since she was pregnant.

"I was lucky that my sister kept one of her puppies, and I kept one, too. They all got to see each other on a regular basis.

"She was quite a lady on her walks and it amazed me.

"My animals, as my children, are allowed on the furniture. I don't care what other humans think about that because many don't realize that animals are intelligent beings with thoughts and feelings. But even though I allowed it, Crystal did not get on the furniture or the bed.

"I wasn't trying to poke into her painful past. I had already guessed about that from her behavior, and I believe that was why she did not play. Although I encouraged her to play because she was only two when I got her, she wouldn't.

"However, I have this feeling that she may have reincarnated and cannot sleep nights having that feeling. If she has, I want to find her. This is why I am looking for help."

Betty's beliefs about reincarnation are shared by many animal communicators worldwide, and I continued the conversation by telling her that dogs do reincarnate, adding that her precious pet definitely remembered her.

"It's not possible she forgot the life you led together and the kindness you showed, Betty.

"I am tuning in to find out if she has reincarnated and I am hearing that indeed she has, and twice. She's been through one quick lifetime and is on her second. A young dog now, she looks quite different. I am seeing a black puppy and suspect it's a Labrador retriever.

"She says she's living a privileged life this time, with no abuse. She does seem to have had a hard time at birth, though, becoming stuck in the birth canal and experiencing a loss of oxygen. As a result, she's not exceptionally bright, just very simple, but happily moving through this current lifetime."

Being attached to competence and always wanting to do a superior job left me with questions about my interpretive skills. Crystal had showed me a red rubber ball. Her beloved human companion had tried to get her to play, yet was unsuccessful. What was the dog trying to tell her? Betty's session taught me that receiving the picture correctly is only half the battle. Figuring out what the picture means is equally important in offering accurate telepathic communication services.

Since that time I've read about and often experienced this issue with people in my workshops. They usually receive a clear picture from animal volunteers, but deciding what it means often takes a collaborative effort between psychic and caretaker.

The feeling of an impact in Crystal's case could have been a metaphor for her abusive situation and not a descriptive image about her death. When I offer general information like that in a session, for example a dog being taken on walks, people often think it's an easy message to bring forward.

"Every dog goes for walks," they say, or "Every cat perches on the back of the couch," but that's not true. Many dogs are in desperate need of exercise and crave going out for a walk, and many cats don't get up on the back of the couch.

For those of us who want to do good work that serves others, especially through controversial services like psychic counseling, holding on to our truth and our own confidence in the face of questioning is a challenge.

*   *   *

Another animal reading in which I found the reaction of the person startling was with a sweet sensitive greyhound by the name of Gracey. The delicate dog was in the depths of grief following the death of her son and she hadn't eaten anything for several days. Her caretaker was extremely worried and called me in to see if I could help. Since Gracey had no body fat at all, even a few days without food could be critical.

After grieving with the dog and letting her know we understood how difficult this time was for her, I asked her if there were any kind of food she was willing to eat that could help restore her energy. She showed me a picture of raw liver.

As the session came to an end, her human told me she actually had some liver in the refrigerator. With Gracey in tow the three of us went to the refrigerator, pulled out the liver, and offered Gracey a piece. She ate it immediately.

"Oh well, all dogs love liver, but I don't give it to them since it's rich and gives them the runs," said Gracey's person. She completely missed the accurate communication, diagnosis, and miraculous result of the information the greyhound had transmitted. This happens most often with canine experts who feel they should have had the resolution to a problem.

These are the times when I've re-examined whether my Higher Sources want me to continue with this work and if I'm good enough to do it. Facing the fear and moving forward anyway is what I've been called to do. What keeps me going is a consistent message from my Guides when I'm having doubts.

"Are you sure I'm on the right track?" I ask Heaven.

Within minutes the phone rings, and it's another person

asking for help.

That's as clear a message as they send. ☼

40

A Cautionary Tale

Lynn's life was a good one. She was content without a boyfriend for the time being, and her family life was one of harmony and love. She enjoyed her job but was considering moving in another career direction. On a whim, she consulted a psychic to find out if there was anything to be concerned about in the near future. She expected only entertainment and a confirmation that a seer shared her good feelings.

But the psychic told Lynn she could see a dark cloud over her head. It seemed to follow Lynn around, the psychic said, with dark spirits attached to it. She predicted illness, treachery, death, and loss in Lynn's immediate future. With this frightening and gloomy picture, Lynn panicked. To add insult to injury, the psychic charged Lynn $250 in exchange for filling her with dread and fear during the short session.

Lynn called me to find out if I would predict the same dreadful events.

"I phoned you because you gave me a very accurate reading a year and a half ago, and as I recall, it was reasonably priced," she said. "I want to know what you see in my future."

"Thank you for calling," I replied. "It's always fulfilling to have repeat clients.

"I'm going to begin by looking at your career change. When I tune in to this change, it feels exciting. I believe you're following the correct path. The job coming up for you will be challenging, but once you learn the ropes, you're going to love it.

"The man you will make your life partner is still out there, but he is a year and a half away," I told her.

I let her know I would check over her health next by performing a body scan—taking a look at her ethereal form and scanning it from head to toe.

"Your health looks good. I don't see any blocks in your

system when I do the body scan, but watch out for a possible knee injury. It feels like a strain or a pull of some kind, but nothing too serious. I see you jogging, and I would recommend something with a little less impact for a short time—maybe two weeks."

Lynn confirmed that although her knee had been a little achy, she had ignored her body's warnings and continued jogging. At the same time, she had been considering trying a different exercise routine.

Then she expressed disappointment that her life mate was still so far away.

"Last time you gave me a reading, you said he would show up in two years. It's been almost that long now, and I was hoping that he would be here any day," she said ruefully.

"Okay. Let's change history then," I told her. "Free will is always operating. We can alter this timeline anytime you are ready to manifest your mate. Of course, he has to be ready too, but you are never locked into a predestined timeline. Let's decide today that he will show up in the next three months.

"If we both maintain this as a strong conviction, and you have done your work on releasing all the blocks to making this happen, and he also becomes ready in the next three months, then you are not stuck with any timeline that I have predicted in the past."

We had a good laugh and then visualized Lynn's mate showing up within the three-month time frame. I also made sure she had a good picture of what he was like. She had really done her homework on that, describing her top five most important characteristics with ease:

"He's had a good family life and he's also honest, loyal, and has a sense of humor. He's politically liberal and a strong environmentalist."

"Definitely do-able," I said. "Nothing unreasonable there, and no reason you can't manifest that."

As our session continued and Lynn became more comfortable, she confided that the psychic she consulted the previous week had offered to remove the dark cloud of treachery above her head for a significant fee.

"Whoa, Nelly! Big red flag," I said. "That's a textbook sign that the psychic you're dealing with has no integrity."

"I wondered about that," Lynn said.

As our session came to an end, I asked her to tell me more about the events I'd predicted 18 months before.

She recalled the 15-minute session that had taken place with me at a psychic fair in San Diego, when I had seen men all around her.

"I have five people in my life, all men," she had told me.

During the session, she had named each one, along with his geographic location, and I had accurately described their personalities and some challenges they faced.

I had also predicted that for a short time she would date two men who were looking for a mother figure.

"I did," she said. "I think they were Richard and Aaron. You also told me that the man I had been dating, who I recently broke up with, would regret the separation in five years. And that he was afraid of being in the dating world as a sexual being. He certainly did have issues in that area."

*   *   *

Following up with Lynn a few months after our phone session, I was pleased to hear that her career change had gone smoothly except for the period of transition and re-training. As predicted, she struggled with learning her new job, but once it was mastered she started to really enjoy the work. She had felt lost for a short time, but she recalled our session and knew the feelings of discomfort would soon pass.

When I last spoke to her, she was awaiting the arrival of her soul mate and feeling much happier being on her own, a clear sign that a significant mate would show up. She had stopped looking for him—the perfect thing to allow the space for the relationship to happen. I had a good, solid, secure feeling of contentment when I tuned into her future. ☀

41

Working With An Animal Communicator

As I've indicated earlier, interpreting the messages your animal companion may send you often requires a bit of "playing charades" to pinpoint details. It can also involve collaborating with an animal communicator who can help you "translate" information, as well as consulting with other professionals.

Here are some guidelines to help you get the most out of your sessions with a professional animal communicator:

1. All animal communicators have areas of specialty.

Some communicators are classically trained within the medical model and are expert at pinpointing exact body organs and systems that seem problematic. For these kinds of issues, cooperation with your veterinarian is recommended.

In my case, I can offer clients information about a general area of the body that's clogged or achy, even naming the liver or kidney area, for example. I can also remotely view foods and medicine to predict how the animal would feel after ingesting these substances. I can also look at areas like the digestive system, the elimination system, or the skeletal system. My services include looking out from an animal's perspective and experience how he or she is seeing, hearing, and sensing the outside world. Many older animals show me that they can see only 50 percent of what they used to be able to see.

All communicators should be able to answer questions and provide information about how your animal is feeling health-wise or how he or she feels about suggested medical procedures or medications.

2. Animal communicators can work effectively from a remote distance, and many offer services by phone.

Since telepathic communication has no limitation when it comes to time, space, or geographic distance, phone readings are just as effective as in-person visits. Sitting quietly with a picture of an animal yields a flow of information for the professional communicator, void of the anxieties or distractions of the animal's caretaker. After the connection is made by phone, that impetus of clarity continues.

3. Your animal companion will not divulge anything that is confidential.

Your animal will not offer much information if you are a very private person, unless you yourself pose specific questions to the communicator. Your session will elicit information from the animal that you already sensed (usually), new things you didn't know (often), and messages from the heart (always).

4. Keep an open mind during your session to allow for the animal's perspective.

What you "hear" from your animal companion will include what is best for the animal's evolution and may differ from your plans. As you receive messages through an animal communicator, allow your animal companion to have his or her own point of view. Respect for the animal is a prerequisite to resolving any problem issues. Allow him or her to say no to your plans.

5. Animals often communicate with behaviors we don't like because they are non-verbal.

These problematic behaviors are always trying to tell us something. Sometimes actions like inappropriate chewing, scratching, or urinating reflect turmoil within the *human* household.

6. In general, animals cannot be "talked out of" behaving instinctively.

Some animals will strike a deal with you to modify instinctual urges, but an animal's ability to achieve this varies. Locked out of my friend's house until she returned with a key an hour later, I had asked her Akita to unlatch the door. "Can't do it," the dog told me, even though we both knew and trusted each other. "It's totally against my protective nature."

Another very common example is when animals are intuitively driven to die alone but their humans want to be holding them at the time of transition. This can be negotiated, but it's a serious bargaining chip for an animal to go against its instinct of seeking out a dark, quiet, completely private place in which to exit its body.

7.   Some information coming from an animal communicator may not make *immediate* sense.

Allow the information to settle, think about it, and in time it will probably make sense.

8.   Even the best psychics and animal communicators are only human.

A good psychic or animal communicator is about 85 percent accurate, so please allow for this small margin of error. Also, remember that predictions are offered to you of your *future probable reality* viewed from this moment in time. With free will operating, paths are fluid and changeable.

Finally, be aware that not all animal communicators adhere to a professional code of ethics. But I do, and I'm proud to be one of those listed in the directory maintained by animal communication pioneer Penelope Smith. Before signing on, communicators agree to comply with a code of ethics. I've personalized it to fit the agreement I make in my work with people and their animals:

For the Highest Good of All Concerned

1.   We promote the idea of the spiritual interconnectedness of all beings, compassionate action amongst all beings, and the raising of consciousness toward healing our planet.

2.   We honor the inherent value and equality of all life, human and nonhuman.

3.   We support the advancement of each being's honorable goals and purposes.

4.   We honor and promote the innate capacity of nonhuman

and human animals to communicate with each other.

5. We commit to using communication for the greatest and highest good of all when that good is for nurturing rather than exploitation.

6. We support the qualities of depth, perceptiveness, and spiritual essence of nonhuman and human animals through communication with each other, and through respect, reverence, and compassionate treatment.

7. We believe that animals must be allowed to exist and function within their own natural lifestyle, wild or domestic, according to their own goals and purposes without interference, except for interventions to rescue and rehabilitate. The intent is to return them to their environment whenever possible.

8. We believe that humans have a responsibility to protect animals from human-imposed suffering, and to enhance their rights and well-being through compassionate action.

9. We believe in the rights of animals to complete their earthly journey in respect, care, safety, balance, health, joy, peace, and love. We believe in relieving them of suffering through humane euthanasia.

10. We believe in emotional sustenance through life-centered community with others of like values and beliefs.

11. We value service grounded in a balance of self-assurance and humble respect.

12. We commit to maintaining understanding, respect, and compassion toward all participants.

13. We believe learning takes place primarily through encouraging, promoting, supporting, and reinforcing strengths, as well as respectfully and compassionately correcting errors.

14. We commit to establishing an atmosphere of safety where mistakes may occur to be used as learning tools.

15. We honor the integrity of our work by maintaining ethics and standards of excellence to guide training, services, and life-centered community, and by applying our skills conscientiously.

16. We provide to clients honest, accurate, timely, complete, and compassionate consultations.

17. We believe in taking compassionate action toward humans and animals as individuals and as groups within the limits and strengths of our own capabilities, intervening and taking action to address problems whenever possible.

18. We believe in leading our lives with compassionate intention directing daily actions.

— Sections taken from the Assisi Institute
www.assisianimals.org

42

How To Talk to Animals

We all have the innate ability to communicate with animals. In fact, we do it all the time. People chat with their pets just by thinking thoughts that automatically send pictures to animals. If you have any doubt about whether you talk to your pet now, just *think* about giving your dog or cat a bath or taking a walk and watch what happens.

But to do this consciously and effectively, become aware of your thoughts and the mental pictures you are sending to your animal companion.

Chatting with your dog or cat is simple, but it's not easy, and it takes practice both to send and to receive messages. Here is a seven-step process to get you started:

1. Get clear
Begin with a meditation that will give you a calm and tranquil mind, and seek out a pleasing and tranquil atmosphere for you and your animal.

2. Ask for help
Ask your Teachers and Guides to help you with this process.

3. Engage your pet
Say your animal's name telepathically to get his or her attention, and visualize your animal as you say his or her name.

4. Start sending pictures
Send a picture of your pet's physical body to him or her, along with your pet's name.

5. Request information

Ask if there is anything your pet would like you to do for him or her. Imagine your animal is sending an answer back to you through a picture, thought, sound, smell, or feeling. Your imagination is powerful—accept whatever you receive, even if it seems nonsensical. (You might get a bunch of grapes when an iguana is telling you she is pregnant. But iguana eggs cluster in small green bunches.)

6. Trust what you get

Always acknowledge the answers to your questions and thank your Guides and the animal for their willingness to communicate with you in this way.

7. Keep practicing

Continue to ask your pet other questions and trust the ongoing images. Remember that it takes practice to sort your own thoughts from the messages being sent to you by the animal.

*   *   *

When I am traveling to a location, I telepathically let the animals know that a person is on the way who knows how to hear their messages telepathically. I can feel a sort of excitement from them as I approach the property. The same thing happens when I know I will have a phone session.

Many people report that their pet comes close and stays next to them just prior to the session, or acts differently in the hours preceding a session—more excited, more attentive, etc. Following a session, the most prevalent report I get from animal caretakers is that their animals are more calm and relaxed.

An excellent time to communicate with animals is when they are sleeping. Sometimes people want to wake a pet or go find it and bring it into the room, but I discourage this. Animals feel threatened by direct eye contact—notice how they often look away when you look directly at them. In the animal world, direct eye contact can be threatening when accompanied by other behavioral signals.

Sometimes I feel that animals are communicating with me directly. Other times I feel that there is an intermediary (the animals' Soul Leader or my Soul-level Guides). I believe the reason for this variation is that animals range from very simple to very intelligent, and some are better communicators than others.

Usually I tune in to an animal's situation, then "show" it to the animal and feel in my body how he or she feels about it emotionally.

One woman I remember distinctly saw me about her sensitive Australian shepherd, a natural herding dog who could not seem to get sheepherding exactly right. The dog had already spent months in training with some of the best in the business. The woman was disappointed and highly critical of the dog because she expected great things from his breeding.

I relayed the message that what her dog wanted most was approval and acceptance. He just didn't like herding sheep and became overheated doing it. His caretaker didn't believe what I was saying so she consulted another animal communicator who told her what she wanted to hear, namely, that the dog was competitive and would be a good herder with the right training. The woman immediately enrolled her dog into a school where yet another expert trainer was also unable to produce the results she wanted.

Subsequently the dog's caretaker attended an animal communication class in which her dog's picture was shown to the students for their impressions. Without any prompting from me, their comments included things like "He's overheated," "He doesn't like doing this," "He's not competitive," and "He'd prefer a different activity."

The woman's response to the class input was to hire a new trainer for her Australian shepherd. The dog was miserable when I checked on him and his caretaker continued to be disappointed—and several hundred dollars poorer, too.

*   *   *

When I say communicating with animals is simple but not easy, I mean it takes dedication, practice, and a clear mind in order to be successful.

As in any professional pursuit, it takes time to master the art of telepathy. The best animal communicators, psychics, and telepaths spend at least some time every day in meditation and prayer. Asking our Higher Sources for guidance and clearing the mind and body of blockages and outside noise, chatter, and interference is part of what should be an everyday process for the professional.

Professional pet psychics also advise people and they should have counseling skills as well. Since my practice began with psychic counseling for people, I now offer psychic counseling for people and animals, and my clients benefit from one-stop shopping! ☀

Listening to Animals

— Sally O. Walshaw, M.A., V.M.D.
College of Veterinary Medicine
Michigan State University

Although animals cannot speak, they certainly do communicate with each other. A person can "listen" to an animal's body language, monitor bodily functions, and assess the animal's well-being. But there is more to this than simple observations. To "listen" well to an animal, the person should indulge in anthropomorphism. One must put oneself in the animal's place and imagine what it would be like to be an animal in various situations, e.g., recovering from surgery, experiencing cancer pain, feeling the discomfort of a fever. Putting oneself in the animal's place (even the cage of a tiny mouse) can help us decide what is the right thing to do for the animal.

Some animals and some species (especially prey animals) tend to conceal their illnesses. One must "listen" very carefully for subtle indications of pain or illness in these animals. Some animals are stoic while others of the same species are very sensitive to pain. We must not discount the pain of one animal because another animal does not react the same way.

"Listening" to animals requires imagination and some guesswork. But if done carefully, it affords the best chance to provide ethical approaches to the complicated questions of animal care and use.

— *Medical Humanities Report*, Center for
Ethics and Humanities in the Life Sciences,
Volume 20, No. 3, Spring 1999

43

Training Tips

The "mind pictures" we can use in communicating with animals not only help them understand what we are trying to tell them and what they want us to know, but they can be helpful when we are trying to teach a pet what is acceptable and unacceptable behavior.

Many people are reluctant to discipline their pets, believing that taking action to change their behavior will send the pet a message that they are unloved. But the opposite is true. Pets need and like boundaries, just like children.

Dogs generally understand only very simple spoken language, and that's why trainers suggest using audio signals like clickers, short, sharp sounds, or commands like "sit" and "stay." (Some dogs are the exception. Rico, who showed extraordinary ability retrieving 37 specific toys out of 40 when told to fetch them, was compared to a three-year-old child in language skills by researchers [*Science* 304, p. 1682].)

So when I instruct people to have a dialogue with their pets, it's because I know that their "mind pictures" will follow their spoken language. What animals are picking up from their humans is a specific feeling (for example, approval or disapproval) and telepathic images showing them *You're staying home because you howled in the car.*

Sometimes more active discipline is required. Alpha animals do this all the time by pinning subordinate animals down on the ground until the subordinate animal shows its belly. This technique also works for humans and their pets when trying to tame aggression or change behavior.

For a dog who barks at the door, a quick, sharp sound, or gently pushing on the dog's behind so he sits down, followed by a reward, will work wonders. At the same time, giving the command to "Be calm," or "Be quiet" offers additional verbal cues. As soon as your dog is calm and his body relaxes, don't forget to praise him.

Naturally, you'll need to let the person at the door know you are training your dog and that you will be right there. You can also enlist a friend ahead of time for this exercise, having her ring the bell or knock on the door as you go through this training exercise several times.

This physical technique is not necessary for all dogs. For more sensitive and responsive souls, a sharp rap on the hand with a rolled-up newspaper offers a startling and distracting sound that interrupts and changes the behavior. Smart dogs won't need you to do that very many times before they get the message.

Finally, although it's preferable to reward a dog immediately after good behavior occurs, it isn't always possible. You can give an animal a time-out when you get home if he's chewed up something in the house when you've been at work all day, and he'll get it—partly because while you're scolding him you'll be sending a feeling of being displeased and a mental picture of the chewed-up item. On the other hand, you can't be around the animal all day and then arbitrarily decide to punish him about something he did two hours before.

*   *   *

A combination of telepathic communication and behavioral reinforcement works equally well with cats.

Let's say you have a kitty who is using your bed as a litter box. After confirming that he is not suffering from a bladder infection or other health problem, you can begin communicating your wishes through the seven steps outlined previously.

Proceed by spending at least five or 10 minutes getting clear and focused. Five to 10 deep breaths can completely change your energy and clear out pent-up stresses, so start there. It does not matter where your cat is physically. He's likely to join you in the room you're in as you go forward, but his presence isn't necessary.

Next, move your focus to the third-eye area of your

forehead (just between your eyebrows). Ask your Higher Sources to help you with this communication. Mentally call your pet's name and imagine yourself approaching him with love and respect. Visualize your kitty urinating in the cat box, immediately followed by a vision of praise and affection. (Be sure to keep the picture of your cat peeing on the bed out of your head—this is part of what takes practice).

Thank your Helpers, trust that the communication has gotten through, and also thank your kitty for talking to you.

Now let's say there will be consequences for your kitty if he doesn't quit peeing on the bed. You need to be clear on exactly what those consequences are going to be and then follow through. Will it be 10 minutes in a crate? A day spent in the garage? No Fancy Feast® for two days?

We all know what happens when we threaten children with restrictions or punishment and then never follow through: We lose credibility and the youngsters push their behavior to new heights of disruption to see if we're really serious. Well, it's no different with pets.

Having said that, it's far more effective to use positive reinforcement than it is to use consequences. Praise your kitty up and down, back and forth, whenever he uses the litter box correctly.

In the most critical litter box cases, people tell me they will have to give the cat up if the problems continue. If that's the case, follow steps one through four and then send your cat a telepathic picture of him going to the shelter, being handed over to a person there, and looking out from inside a cage. Follow that up with a vision of him either finding a new home or undergoing euthanasia. Offer these visions in as loving an attitude as possible.

Because your telepathic mind pictures will usually follow your spoken words, you can even tell him out loud, "If you keep going on the bed, I will take that as a sign that you want to live somewhere else. I can't be happy in my home if you continue that behavior."

Keep an open mind and trust what happens. When you're just getting started, don't expect miracles after the very first session. The first time, your cat may be surprised that you are talking to him. Give it at least a week.

Hire a professional animal communicator once the vet has cleared your cat of any medical problems. Every cat who is going outside his litter box is trying to tell you something.

Tanker was one such cat. When I tuned in to him, he had a stomachache and a slight case of diarrhea.

"I see three cat boxes in your house and one he has never used," I told Tanker's caretaker. "I feel an allergy problem, both inside and outside his body and I'm being shown that it is corn. Please check the food you are giving Tanker and make sure it doesn't contain corn."

The third cat box was filled with corn-based cat litter, a new product chosen because it was less messy.

As soon as Tanker's food was upgraded to a better quality without corn in it, he started using the box again.

Many people who care for animals become extremely attached, but allowing a cat to pursue what he needs for his own evolution may include leaving the home he has shared with you. The cat may choose to continue peeing on the bed because he needs to live somewhere where he is free to go outside, or he may be telling you that he wants to go on a feral adventure. Cats do this all the time. They are very adventurous creatures and they may leave to explore the neighborhood, the city, or the state.

Don't forget that when you are communicating with animals, they have every right to say, "No thanks." ☀

197

Epilogue

"When we find no support among others for our deeply felt truths, we can either feel isolated and bitter, or celebrate the fact that our vision is strong enough even to survive the powerful human need for approval of family, friends or colleagues."

~ Osho Zen Tarot

Reverence for all life. That's where the animals led me on my evolutionary journey. The purpose of life is to evolve, and the animals I've met have boosted me up a few rungs on the ladder that leads to a higher level of compassion and understanding.

Especially Rusti.

My beloved Rusti died on the day I embarked alone on a full-circle move from the Olympic Peninsula of Washington state back home to California's Central Coast—back to the place where we had found one another. I knew she wouldn't make the trip physically. She told me so.

"Girl," I said, "I can see that two of your legs aren't working very well, your ankles are shot, you're having a helluva time getting comfortable at all, and I can't deny I'm smelling the death breath. When you are ready, please make a small deposit inside the house, and I will take it as a sign that the time for you to move on has come." Two weeks later, she did just that in the hallway. Never before that. Never after that. Just the once. Her message was clear.

Over the next few weeks, she was able to make it across the lawn and out to the road to sniff where the walking dogs had been in the morning, but it was hard for her to get back to the house where two entry steps created an obstacle. She could only take four steps before she tired out completely.

I spooned with her on the floor, whispered sweet words in her fuzzy, perky ears about how much she meant to me, entreated her to contact me from the other side, sang to her, danced for her, and rubbed her sore joints. Calm, contented love, gratitude, and respect poured from my hands into her.

I kissed her soft muzzle and laughed at the remembered image of her when, back in the day, she lay with her head thrown back and her black lips flopping open, revealing a snaggletooth look that was pure comedy. I breathed in the odor of her oily doggie skin, admired her velvety blue-black deep-purple tongue with the quarter-sized pink spot at the back of it, and marveled at the softness of the down fur behind her bear-like ears.

Making arrangements to help Rusti leave her body with my regular veterinarian proved problematic. Having suffered from a nasty and prolonged bout with the flu, she was catching up on a backlog of clients, and I was never able to get an appointment with her. Time ran out and I found another vet willing to help us at the last minute.

Our appointment was at 11 a.m. that day. Pillows, blankets, and propped-up bedding transformed the front passenger seat into a doggie limo bed that would transport Rusti to her final physical destination. But those miles of comfortable bedding did not fully mitigate her physical discomforts and she was nervous about getting into the car. By then, we hadn't ridden together for months, and she squirmed and tried to settle down during the half-hour ride.

"Stay, girl," I told her as I parked and exited the car. My husband squeezed out of the back seat behind me so together we could lift her 54 pounds out from the passenger side of the car.

Attached to a long leash, she ambled off to pee in a dusty road construction site outside the veterinarian's office as soon as her feet touched the ground. I waited patiently, then gently guided her inside.

The floors were wood, shellacked to a high gloss and slick. A carpet runner the length of the waiting-room floor gave Rusti some leverage, but her giant pillow was not there and she could not get comfortable on the hard floor. She would attempt to sit or lie down, only to get up immediately and move along. For the next 30 minutes, as we waited, she paced the length of the room, traveling maybe a quarter of a mile. She hadn't moved that much for months.

"Suzan and Rusti," the assistant called out from the back. Rusti, completely tuckered out, took one baby step at a time toward the back as we proceeded to a small room that looked like a storage area.

"Come on girl," I reassured her. "It's gonna be all right." My husband and an assistant hoisted her onto a stainless steel table that protruded from a sink behind it. It had a steel grate that separated the dog from the smoother metal underneath.

Rusti's back end was positioned over a sink.

The hard metal made me wince. Although the staff was caring and concerned, this was not the comfortable crossing-over scene I had imagined for us. But my stoic girl was lifted onto the grate, and lay on her belly as they readied the electric razor.

"So Rusti is a chow chow about 13 years old?" the vet asked me.

"Yes," I said, glancing up from Rusti's eyes to check out where they were in the proceedings.

The vet's assistant shaved a small place on Rusti's forearm and searched for veins.

"She looks fantastic. It's really a testament to how you have cared for her," the vet said kindly.

The assistant inserted a shunt.

"It goes pretty fast once the solution is injected," said the vet, "so I recommend people focus on their animal and be completely present with them from here on out."

I took his advice. With my lips brushing her soft rust-white muzzle, I breathed her in for the last time, enveloping her on a soul level. I said, "You have been the greatest dog in the world, girl, and I will never stop loving you. Don't be afraid. I love you soooo much, my little red dog. You're the best and I will miss you. See you on the other side, my sweet doggie-girl."

The vet and his assistant spoke softly to one another.

"Okay," I heard him say.

The light slowly faded from Rusti's eyes as the medicine went in.

*   *   *

I left Rusti's body in the care of the vet and took her spirit with me. But I was keenly aware of the physical separation.

Within the hour I was at the wheel of a three-day drive home, leaving my husband behind temporarily in his job. After five and a half years, I was finally moving back to the place where my heart lived. The place where my two-cat family had morphed into a two-cat/one-dog family, and where I had first been introduced to animal communication.

I talked to Rusti the entire trip. We laughed. We cried. We celebrated. We rejoiced at the first sightings of the Pismo

Dunes and the Pacific Ocean where she had loved to roll in the sand. We vowed to keep in touch.

After that, it seemed to me that Rusti necessarily retreated for about six weeks. I respected her space. (Dogs, like humans, go through a reassessment period after death and are out of touch, usually for at least a couple of weeks. Then their ability to communicate can be assisted by a myriad of heavenly helpers, or sometimes they are skilled enough to communicate themselves after death.)

Rusti did not stay gone forever. My girl eventually reappeared as a happy puppy in my dreams. When I feel sad or when I miss her embodied self, one particular reflection gives me reassurance: I know that I could not have loved her more, nor could I have treated her better.

These days I still request that Rusti share her wisdom with me in my work. On particularly difficult cases where the answers seem elusive, I ask her if she'll help me find a resolution for the animal and its person. "Weigh in, girl. I'm listening." I've no doubt she is one of a cast of angels that assist me in my work.

Dispatches from the Ark is about my life as an empath. It's the story of a sacred gift enabling me to feel what an animal feels, to see pictures of their experiences from their points of view, and to translate these into words that promote greater interspecies harmony.

As a translator link between the seen and the Divine Unseen, I'm proud to be part of a community of animal communicators, caregivers, and rescuers affiliated with Penelope Smith's pioneering work, workshops, and publications, all of which are professionalizing the field.

Working within a code of ethics, these professional interspecies communicators are Spirit-filled people of integrity who are well-intended, talented, knowledgeable—and divinely inspired. ☀

References and Recommended Reading

Conversations with Animals: Cherished Messages and Memories as Told by an Animal Communicator, Lydia Hiby. Troutdale, Ore. (1998)

Coping With Sorrow on the Loss of Your Pet (2nd Edition), Moira Anderson Allen, M. Ed. Morris Publishing (2004)

Developing Intuition: Practical Guidance for Daily Life, Shakti Gawain. Novato, Calif.: Nataraj Publishing (2000)

"Did Animals Sense A Tsunami Was Coming?" Maryann Mott. National Geographic News (Jan. 4, 2005)

Kinship With All Life, J. Allen Boone. New York, N.Y.: Harper & Row (1954)

The Pet Psychic: What the Animals Tell Me, Sonya Fitzpatrick. New York, N.Y.: Berkley Books (2003)

Straight From the Horse's Mouth: How To Talk to Animals and Get Answers, Amelia Kinkade. New York, N.Y.: Crown Publishers (2001)

The Tellington TTouch: A Revolutionary Natural Method to Train and Care for Your Favorite Animal, Linda Tellington-Jones and Sybil Taylor. New York, N.Y.: Viking Penguin (1992)

What The Animals Tell Me, Beatrice Lydecker. New York, N.Y.: Harper & Row Publishers (1977)

About the Author

Suzan Vaughn has devoted her life to every form of communication, including print, broadcast, and telepathic media. As a broadcast journalist for more than two decades in Southern and Central California, she wrote and reported for radio, television, and print media before switching careers to become a registered telepathic counselor for people and their pets.

Vaughn helps clients on the phone, in person, and through her Web site at *www.telepathictalk.com*. With a professional background that includes thousands of hours behind the microphone and in front of the camera, she is an excellent media-friendly guest with a proven track record of popular multimedia appearances. As a writer, she has published newspaper articles, feature stories, radio and television news scripts, and pet psychic columns in two magazines.

Vaughn's psychic work has been profiled in the nationwide magazine *Species Link* and in California's *Coast Magazine*, as well as in Washington state newspapers like *The Sequim Gazette* and *The Daily World* (Raymond). She has appeared as a guest on XM Satellite Radio's "Good Morning America Take Five Show with Hillarie Barsky," "The Dave Congalton Show" (KVEC Radio, San Luis Obispo, California), KXLY-TV 4 (Spokane), and other venues.

Vaughn holds a B.A. degree in psychology and an M.A. in communication from California State University, Fullerton, and has studied metaphysical teachings for more than 25 years. In 2001, at the age of 45, she met her husband, Bob, on the Internet, married for the first time, and started a new life on the Olympic Peninsula, subsequently relocating to San Luis Obispo.

Vaughn enjoys traveling and is available for extensive promotional touring. Through modest philanthropy, she empowers women who are victims of war, animals who are abused or abandoned, and families who can use a micro loan to establish a business. ❁

Made in the USA
Monee, IL
03 September 2022

12492250R00125